Praise for *With Custer on the Little Bighorn*

"A substantial addition to the scant oeuvre."
—*The Boston Globe*

"Thoroughly exciting and authentic."
—*Parade Magazine*

"Adds to what we know about all the battles in the Indian wars."
—*Men's Journal*

"In clear, straightforward prose, Taylor vividly evokes the disastrous
battle. . . . The book makes fascinating reading for all those interested
in the Army's most famous defeat."
—*Houston Chronicle*

"Has the ring of authenticity."
—*Richmond Times-Dispatch*

"Certain to be cited from now on."
—*The Dallas Morning News*

"A volume that will delight Custer buffs and engage scholars of the campaign.
Vivid and original firsthand accounts of both the confused retreat of Reno's
battalion across the Little River and the grisly process of identifying
already decomposing corpses on the site of the Last Stand."
—*Publishers Weekly*

"More than a battlefield epic. This sweeping account by a surprisingly gifted
writer . . . is a vibrant, living history that easily leaps the 120-year chasm
between us and combatants that day at the Little Bighorn."
—*Kirkus Reviews*

*   *   *

Greg Martin, a leading collector and expert on Western lore, bought the
William O. Taylor manuscript and memorabilia that came with it in 1995.
He lives in San Fancisco.

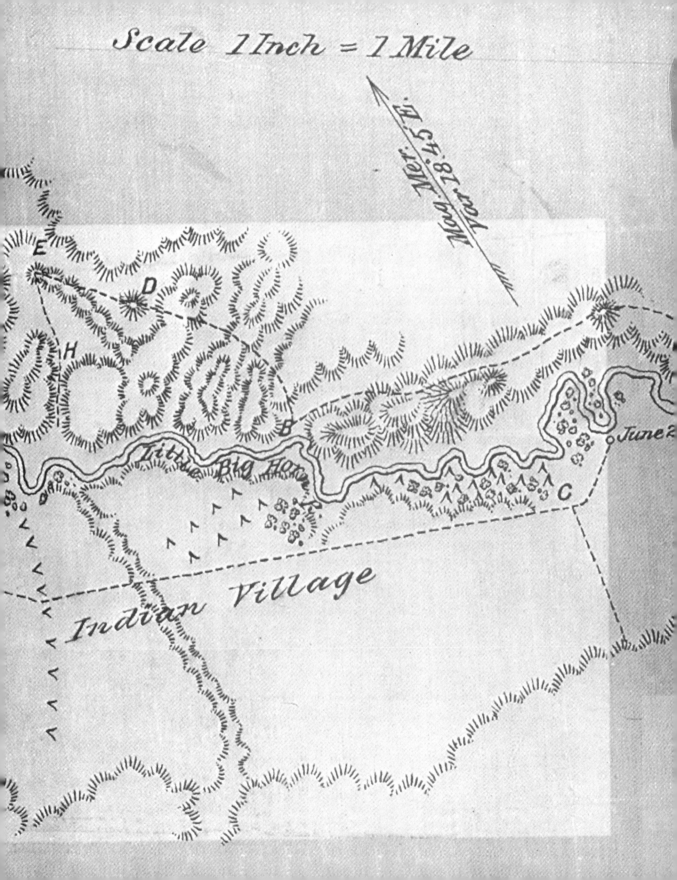

Scale 1 Inch = 1 Mile

Mag Mer. 78°45′ E.
Var. 18°

E
D
H
B
Little Big Horn
Indian Village
C
June 2

Encampment

Benteen's
March

Reno's Crossing

A

Plan of the Battlefield
on the Little Big Horn Creek
Dakota Territory
June 25th 1876
By Lt. E. Maguire Corps of Engineers
to accompany his preliminary Report
to the Chief of Engineers
Dated July 2nd 1876

To the heroes and heroines of the Old West

who have enriched my life in many ways

With Custer on the Little Bighorn

THE FIRST—AND ONLY—
EYEWITNESS ACCOUNT
EVER WRITTEN

WILLIAM O. TAYLOR

Foreword by Greg Martin

PENGUIN BOOKS

PENGUIN BOOKS
Published by the Penguin Group
Penguin Books USA Inc., 375 Hudson Street, New York, New York 10014, U.S.A.
Penguin Books Ltd, 27 Wrights Lane, London W8 5TZ, England
Penguin Books Australia Ltd, Ringwood, Victoria, Australia
Penguin Books Canada Ltd, 10 Alcorn Avenue, Toronto, Ontario, Canada M4V 3B2
Penguin Books (N.Z.) Ltd, 182–190 Wairau Road, Auckland 10, New Zealand

Penguin Books Ltd, Registered Offices: Harmondsworth, Middlesex, England

First published in the United States of America by Viking Penguin,
a division of Penguin Books USA Inc. 1996
Published in Penguin Books 1997

1   3   5   7   9   10   8   6   4   2

Photographs on pages ii, xv, 3, 6, 22, 28, 29, 33, 39, 40, 43, 49, 66, 77, 102, 112, 120, 124,
128, 143, 150, 156, 157, 207, Greg Martin Collection

Photographs on pages 16, 19, 36, 42, 74, 76, 78, 79, 80, 85, 86, 146, 148, 158,
© Butterfield & Butterfield

Map by Lieutenant E. McGuire, National Archives and Records Service

THE LIBRARY OF CONGRESS HAS CATALOGUED THE HARDCOVER AS FOLLOWS:
Taylor, William O., 1855–1923.
With Custer on the Little Bighorn: a newly discovered first-person account/
by William O. Taylor; foreword by Greg Martin.
p.   cm.
Includes bibliographical references.
ISBN 0-670-86803-5 (hc.)
ISBN 0 14 02.5576 1 (pbk.)
1. Taylor, William O., 1855–1923.   2. Little Bighorn, Battle of the, Mont., 1876—Personal
narratives.   3. United States. Army. Cavalry, 7th—Biography.   4. Soldiers—United
States—Biography.   5. Custer, George Armstrong, 1839–1876.   I. Title.
E83.876.T39   1996
973.8´2—dc20   95–52413

Printed in the United States of America
Set in Janson Text
Designed by Jaye Zimet

The event that ultimately led to my discovery of William O. Taylor's memoir of the battle of the Little Bighorn occurred on a summer day in 1952 while I was accompanying my mother in a quest for antique furniture.

Just outside of San Francisco we stopped at a dilapidated junk store. Upon entering, I immediately noticed an old Colt cap-and-ball pistol nailed high on a wall. For some unexplained reason, I was driven to it like a moth to a flame. After a brief negotiation with the proprietress, who quoted a price of fifteen dollars, I held a lengthy discussion with my reluctant mother, who was definitely not enamored of firearms. A compromise was reached. Her twelve-year-old son could buy the pistol if he wished to invest his entire net worth of ten dollars. Without hesitation, an offer was made and accepted by a sympathetic shopkeeper.

Hurrying home, I carefully disassembled and cleaned my newfound treasure, probing its innermost secrets. I delighted in its "click, click" as I pulled the hammer back and watched the cylinder turn. Where had it been, and what adventures had it been a part of, I wondered, as visions of great battles, cowboys, Indians, and desperadoes rushed through my mind.

After studying several books and catalogs that I had sent away for, I learned that my old Colt had been made during the Civil War, was a rather scarce model, and was of a type carried westward. Furthermore, it was listed as having a value in excess of one hundred dollars.

The excitement of my first profitable acquisition, and the thrill of unraveling its history, caused me not only to devote a disproportionate amount of time during my school years to the buying, selling, and trading of antique guns but to embark upon a collecting odyssey embracing a large spectrum of related Western artifacts.

By 1984, after purchasing the entire contents of a Western museum, I was faced with the daunting task of disposing of a gigantic quantity of collectibles that I neither needed nor had the capacity to store.

I contacted the San Francisco auction house Butterfield & Butterfield and consigned one of the largest collections of Western material ever to go under the hammer.

The sale's success resulted in a lasting relationship with this firm, first as a consignor, then, for the past ten years, as consultant and director of its Arms, Armor and Western Memorabilia Department. It was while I served as consultant that perhaps the most interesting and significant collection discovery of my life occurred.

During the latter part of 1994, I began researching a large and important collection of over 200 Custer- and Indian War–related artifacts that had been consigned to Butterfield & Butterfield by a noted New York art dealer. This well-known collection, the most important such assemblage in private hands, contained such museum pieces as General Custer's personal flags from the Civil War, his sword and uniform insignia, and a pair of vases bearing the likenesses of the general and his wife painted during their honeymoon. Also included in the collection was an important undress campaign shirt, handmade by Elizabeth "Libbie" Custer for her husband during his Black Hills expedition of 1874.[1]

Most of the collection, including the Taylor artifacts, had received much publicity over the years, having been pictured in various catalogs, journals, and books on the battle of the Little Bighorn. But one thing among Taylor's belongings that had escaped notoriety captured my attention. It was a rather unpretentious old black tin box containing his personal papers, newspaper clippings, photos, and Indian relics that he had collected himself, all stacked over a thick, neatly handwritten manuscript complete with chapters, table of contents, and a primitive cardboard binding bearing the intriguing title *With Custer on the Little Bighorn.*

This well-written manuscript detailed not only Taylor's personal experiences in the battle, but a complete history of the event, providing facts and observations never before revealed. Further investigation into the life of William O. Taylor and the origins of his manuscript convinced me that his story was of major significance and deserved wide attention.

In an effort to unravel the mystery of why Taylor's writings had remained unknown for over seventy years, I approached the Memorial Hall Museum at Deerfield. Officials there confirmed having deaccessioned all of

---

1. After Custer's death she gave the shirt to her husband's orderly, from whom it was obtained by Private William O. Taylor, a participant in the battle of the Little Bighorn. Furthermore, there was a group of photos, as well as arrows and other Indian artifacts collected by Taylor at the time of the Custer massacre. All of these items were listed as having been in the Memorial Hall Museum at Deerfield, Massachusetts.

William O. Taylor's artifact collection in 1986, but they had never heard of the manuscript. The New York art dealer could not remember from whom he had acquired the black tin box and its contents.

Following the museum's suggestion, I contacted the Orange, Massachusetts, Historical Society in Taylor's hometown. The librarian, Mrs. Linda J. Temple, was most accommodating. She had known of the manuscript's existence, but had no knowledge of its whereabouts. She was able, however, to provide me with a biography of Taylor and a list of his descendants. Since he had had no children, living descendants were distant connections and the trail was difficult.

Then one day, while shuffling through Taylor's black box, I came across a letter dated April 30, 1985, addressed to the National Archives in Washington, D.C., requesting information on William O. Taylor's service record. The return address was that of a woman in Connecticut. On a hunch, I called information and was soon speaking to her. The mystery surrounding the manuscript was solved.

Before his death in 1923, Taylor had bequeathed his artifact collection to the Deerfield Museum, retaining his notes and scrapbooks, a portion of which, along with his writings, were placed in the black tin box for safekeeping. He had hoped to make his work public, but had died before seeing his labors come to fruition. His wife, Jessie, carefully guarded his manuscript along with other contents of the box.

Shortly before her death in 1958, Jessie Taylor passed everything on to a distant relative whose husband was in the printing business, hoping, of course, that Taylor's work would be published. This, however, never happened, and the manuscript remained undisturbed for another thirty-five years, until it was sold to the New York art dealer, in whose collection it reposed for ten more years before reaching Butterfield & Butterfield. Convinced of its historical importance, I purchased Taylor's unpublished work at auction in April 1995.

*   *   *

A glimpse into the life of William O. Taylor reveals an innocent recruit caught up in major historic events. Born to a middle-class family in Canandaigua, New York, on February 18, 1855, Taylor sought adventure at the age of seventeen, enlisting in the army at Troy, New York, on January 17, 1872. He was described as five feet one-half inch, of fair complexion, with hazel eyes and brown hair.

After a brief indoctrination into military life, on February 14, 1872, he was assigned to Company M of the Seventh Cavalry, which was commanded by Lieutenant Colonel (formerly General) George A. Custer. After participating in all of Custer's expeditions through the Yellowstone in 1873 and the Black Hills in 1874, Private Taylor in 1876 joined Troop A, under Captain Myles Moylan. In May of that year, riding to the tune of "The Girl I Left Behind Me," he left the parade grounds of command headquarters at Fort Abraham Lincoln, Dakota Territory, along with the entire Seventh Cavalry, to confront the Sioux and the Northern Cheyenne.

On the morning of June 25, after three days of hard riding in hopes of surprising a large camp of hostile Indians, Companies A, M, and G were divided from the main body of the regiment and put under the command of Major Marcus Reno. Reno's contingent of 112 men took one trail, and General Custer's force took another. Reno was soon caught in furious surprise attacks by the Sioux. Vastly outnumbered, the Reno force retreated across the Little Bighorn River.

Here Taylor became a pawn of flawed leadership. Pinned down and without water, Reno's men were eventually reinforced by Captains Benteen and McDougal's troopers, enabling them to hold out for another thirty-six hours against a tenacious Sioux onslaught, until the relief columns of Generals Terry and Gibbon brought the unbelievable news that Custer's command had been annihilated only a short distance away.

In the early morning of June 27, a dazed and shaken Private Taylor, having survived his baptism of fire, was assigned to the burial party charged with the mournful task of tending to his comrades' looted and scattered remains.

Taylor emerged from his ordeal with the realization that he had taken part in a significant event of American history. The memories and impressions of the scorching June days of 1876 would remain with him forever.

Taylor's health, like that of other troopers who suffered from the severity and hardship of the campaign, failed shortly after the battle, resulting in his discharge from the army on January 17, 1877, at Fort Rice, Dakota Territory.

He returned East and settled in Orange, Massachusetts, where he spent the next thirty years working as a metal polisher at the New Home Sewing Machine Company and seeking facts and answers to the growing controversy as to how the U.S. Army had suffered its greatest defeat in the entire history of its war with the American Indian.

Taylor became an avid student of the battle of the Little Bighorn, and was acquainted and corresponded with many of its participants, as well as with Elizabeth B. Custer. Over the years he added to his relic collection, kept voluminous records detailing accounts taken from newspapers, journals, and books on the subject, and continued to work on his memoir.

He completed his manuscript in 1917, and died five years later, February 19, 1923, at the age of sixty-eight.

Here, generations later, is William O. Taylor's lifelong work, a call from beyond to once again pay homage to that memorable landmark moment in American history.

GREG MARTIN
SAN FRANCISCO, CALIFORNIA

[ACKNOWLEDGMENTS]

The enthusiasm and assistance of others made it possible for me to bring this work to fruition.

First, my gratitude to Jemison Beshears for his valuable contributions, particularly his diligent historical research and insightful annotations of the Custer era and William O. Taylor's writings.

My sincere thanks to Linda J. Temple of the Orange, Massachusetts, Historical Society for her research of the Taylor family genealogy. Special thanks to Ruth F. Hasley, Richard B. Hasley, David Hasley and Stephen Hasley of Simsbury, Connecticut, descendants of William O. Taylor's wife, Jessie, for their endorsement and encouragement. Thanks also to Martin Lane of New York City for providing pertinent material related to William O. Taylor. To Douglas Sandburg for his photographic expertise. To Nancy Padou for her painstaking transcription of William O. Taylor's manuscript. And to my editor, Al Silverman, at Viking Penguin, for his invaluable guidance.

[C O N T E N T S]

Whose was the right and the wrong?

Sing it. oh funeral song,

with a voice that is full of tears.

And say that our broken faith

wrought all this ruin and scathe,

In the year of a Hundred Years.

—H. W. Longfellow

Opposite: The author's
original design for the
cover of his book.

WITH CUSTER

ON

THE LITTLE-BIG-HORN.

[THE ONLY "ADVANCE" REVIEW
OF MR. TAYLOR'S BOOK, AS FOUND
WITHIN THE MANUSCRIPT]

A _Splendid_

+almost _classic_

account of this

fam_ous batt_le It should

have a wide circulation

William Parker

Indian War Veteran

U.S. Army

Northampton, Mass.

Dec. 20th 1923

Preface

It is not my purpose in the following pages to attempt any exhaustive or critical narrative of General Custer's last campaign, but merely to record what I saw of certain events in connection therewith, and the impression they made upon me. This work, a most unfamiliar one, has been undertaken with many misgivings, and a few words of explanation are due both to the author and the reader.

Enlisting into the Regular Army in 1872 and serving therein for the period of five years it was my fortune to be assigned to the 7th U.S. Cavalry, a regiment that had as its Lieutenant Colonel, George A. Custer, Brevet Major-General of Volunteers, who was one of the most noted and gallant Cavalry officers of the Civil War of 1861-65. The Colonel of the Regiment, Samuel D. Sturgis, another well known officer of the Civil War, was, during the midst of my period of service, absent on detached duty, and the Regiment was therefore under the command of its Lieutenant Colonel, George A. Custer, better known and commonly spoken of as "General" Custer.

"The wide and lonely prairies over which our wagons made a trail that lasted for years, see no more the ghost-like cones of the Indians teepee nor hear the war whoop of the Sioux or the crack of his rifle."

Early in 1873 the Regiment was sent from the Southern States into the Territory of Dakota, then but little more than a wilderness of Indians, wolves and sagebrush, without a settlement on the West side of the Missouri River and but very few on the East side. It was the home of the buffalo and the roving Sioux. Here the Regiment took part in various expeditions and campaigns against the Indians, the last one in which I took part, resulting in the death of General Custer and the swift and unexpected annihilation of half the Regiment by the Sioux and Cheyenne Indians at the memorable battle on the Little Bighorn, Montana, June 25th, 1876.

In this campaign and battle the author took part and the impressions made on his memory by the attendant events are ineffaceable, aided perhaps by a half consciousness at the time of the great significance of the events transpiring under his eyesight and knowledge. It was a consciousness and interest that resulted in the immediate beginning of a collection of newspaper clippings and other data that related to the battle, a course of action that has continued for many years, and the result, with my own observations and experiences, have been compiled with the hope of preserving for history and posterity the story of Custer's last battle, as seen by one who was there on his last campaign.

Better pens than mine may tell the story of the Little Bighorn but none will attempt it with a greater personal interest or a more sincere desire to truthfully picture the stirring events, the principal part of which has been and ever will be shrouded with a great veil of mystery, for the last rally and entire destruction of Custer's command on that barren ridge has no parallel in all the annals of our Indian Wars.

The majority of those that took a part in this campaign have passed away and with them has gone much valuable data which should have been preserved. While a great deal has been written in a general way concerning the momentous events in the far Northwest during our centennial year, I find but one portrayal by a participant in the Battle of the Little Bighorn and that one lacked sharing in the opening of the battle by Major Reno.

Some of the events have never received even passing attention from historians and remain today practically unknown. In the things I did not actually see I have tried to exercise due care and present no record but what I believe, from my own experience and general knowledge of the matter, to be the most likely and truthful that has, or can be given. In this class I include a part of the Indians' own story as told by James McLaughlin in *My Friend the*

of Indians, wolves, and Sage brush, without a settlement on the
west side of the Missouri river and but very few on the East side.
the home of the Buffalo and the roving Sioux. here the Regiment
took part in various expeditions and campaigns against the Indians
the last one in which I took part, resulting in the death of
General Custer and the swift and unexpected annihilation of one
half of the Regiment by the Sioux and Cheyenne Indians at the
memorable battle on the Little-Big-Horn, Mont- June 25th 1876.
In this Campaign and battle the author took part and the
impressions made on his memory by the attendant events
are ineffaceable, aided perhaps by a half consciousness at the
time of the great significence of the events transpiring under
his eyesight, and knowledge, a consciousness and intrest that
resulted in the immediate begining of a collection of Newspaper clippings and other data that related to the battle,
A course of action that has continued for many years,
and the result, with my own observations and experiences
have been compiled with the hope of preserving for history
and posterity the story of Custer's last battle, as seen by

Indian. Likewise a sketch of the Indians' charge from The Way of the Indian by Frederic Remington. Special acknowledgements are due to Major General Charles F. Roe, Brigadier General Edward S. Godfrey and Brigadier General E. J. McClernand, all of whom, as Lieutenants, were a part of General Terry's Command in 1876.

The wide and lonely prairies over which our wagons made a trail that lasted for years, see no more the ghost-like cones of the Indians teepee nor hear the war whoop of the Sioux or the crack of his rifle. Gone also are the buffalo, elk and antelope and taking their place are herds of browsing cattle, while peaceful homes and thriving towns dot the sites of many of our camping places.

In passing years the plow of the husbandman turns up some human bones; "Indians", he says and drives along, but if he had been curious enough to notice a small soil-encrusted button which lay among the bones he would have seen the "Eagle" found on all Army uniform buttons. Was it one of Sully's men who fell while fighting their way through the Badlands in 1864? Perhaps it was turned up along the Yellowstone and marked the shallow resting place of one of Gibbon's undaunted infantrymen, or one of Custer's hard-riding troopers?

From Fort Rice to Glendive, from the Powder River to Fort Shaw, along the Tongue, Rosebud and Bighorn Rivers lie unknown graves, the remains of many a sturdy "Regular".

"Of all their grim campaigning, no sight or sound remaining,
They wait the great hereafter when the last Assembly comes."[1]

To their memory, as well as those of my comrades who were "mustered out" on that eventful day on the Little Bighorn, these pages are dedicated.

WILLIAM O. TAYLOR
ORANGE MASS. 1917

---

1. From the poem "Ad Finem Fideles," by Guy Wetmore Carryl.

The Little Bighorn

Oh land so far away, oh hills so bleak and gray,
With moist eyes I seem to see that field again today
Where on the ground thick strewn with sage,
my slaughtered comrades lay.

No boots and spurs, no hat or gun, no uniform had they,
But bare as on their natal day the poor hacked bodies lay.
Close by each one some empty shells, naught else was there to show,
how hard they fought till well aimed shot,
from foeman laid them low.

Tis Burke of "E", a comrade said, as with a stifled moan,
A face he turned up to our view, twas one we all had known
"God rest his soul," and, bending low his head,
A neckerchief he laid upon the bruised face of the dead,
A little earth, some brush of sage, and Burke was left to lie,
scant burial then for anyone, the living soon must fly.

When the roses bloom again along the river,
And the war cry of the Sioux is hushed for aye,
as in days of Auld ang Syne I'll be with you comrades mine,
on the Little Bighorn River, far away.

—William O. Taylor

FIG. 338.—Signal of discovery or alarm.

The Cause of It

The promptings of a love for historical research, strongly emphasized by the fact of personal knowledge and connection with some of the events herein described, coupled with a desire to raise a little corner of the dark curtain of mystery which has shrouded that pathetic field where Custer fell and my comrades died, are the motives that led to the unfamiliar task of recording the sights I witnessed, and the impressions produced while campaigning with Custer on the Little Bighorn.

To go into the causes of the Indian war of 1876, doing justice to the Indians and giving the reader a comprehensive idea thereof, would take far more space, time and ability than I have at my disposal. Suffice it to say that Senate Executive Document, No 9. 2nd Session of the 44th Congress containing "The Report and Journal of Proceedings of the Commission appointed to obtain certain concessions from the Sioux Indians," dated December 18th, 1876, will well repay the reader, and give to the uninformed a fairly good idea of the terrible injustice done the American Indians by the people and government of this country. From this Report I will make use of a few extracts.

In September, 1851, a new treaty was made at Fort Laramie between the United States and certain tribes of Indians, including the Sioux, Cheyennes, Crows and several others residing in what might be called the

Yet often at twilight I fancy
I hear once more that refrain,
"I'd lay me down to die."
And green, ever green in my memory
Are the songs I heard that night
By our Officers sung on the Rosebud
In the twilight before the fight.

— William O. Taylor

Opposite: Signal of Discovery. Inscribed by William O. Taylor as "Quite a little like opening of the Battle of the Little Bighorn June 25 1876."

Northwest section of our country east of the Rocky Mountains. Among other things: " . . . the Government agreed to pay these Indians, the sum of $50,000 for fifty years, the Senate amended the treaty by limiting the appropriations to ten years, this amendment was never submitted to the Indians, they believed that the original treaty was in force . . .". The moment the War of the Rebellion [Civil War] was over thousands of our people turned their attention to the treasures of Montana and the Indian was forgotten. It did not occur to any man that this poor, despised redman was the original discoverer and sole occupant for many centuries. The conflicts which grew out of our bad faith induced Congress to create a commission of representative men from the Army and civil life to establish peace with hostile Indians, ascertain their cause of complaint, and make treaties with them which should remove all causes of war, and protect the frontier settlements. Generals W.T. Sherman, W.T. Harvey, Alfred. H. Terry and C.C. Augur, and messers N.G. Taylor, J.B. Henderson, T.F. Tappen, and J.B. Sanborn, composed that commission. After a most careful examination into the causes of this war, 1866-1868, the gentlemen declare, that "we alone are responsible—."

The Indians were not willing to make another treaty unless they could have the pledge that no white man should ever enter the territory guaranteed to them. The commission consulted the Government and agreed to the conditions required by the Indians. They did more, they pledged, so far as they could do, their solemn faith that this treaty should be observed. We need not recapitulate the provisions of the treaty. It guaranteed the Indians' right to hunt in the Powder river country, and pledged the aid needed by a nomadic race, and made provisions for those who remained on the Reservation, to aid them in the work of civilization. This treaty, after a full knowledge of the facts preserved in the report, was ratified by the Senate and approved by President Grant. Every sentiment of honor, justice, and kindness demanded that it should be faithfully observed.

The ordinance, passed for the government of the territory Northwest of the Ohio river, July, 1787, declares that the utmost good faith shall always be observed toward the Indians, their lands and property shall never be taken from them without their consent, and in their property, rights, and liberty they shall never be invaded or disturbed, unless in just and lawful war authorized by Congress.

In 1874, acting under the orders of General Sheridan, General Custer made an expedition from Fort Lincoln into the Black Hills. It was done against the protest of the Indians, and in plain, direct violation of the treaty. Gold was discovered, white men flocked to the El Dorado notwithstanding the gross violation of the treaty. No open war ensued, there were instances of conflicts between small bands of Indians and whites, theft and robberies were committed.

In 1875 a Commission was sent out to treat for the surrender of the Black Hills, but failed because they had no authority to offer any sum which would be a just equivalent for their rights in the Black Hills or which gave to the Indians hopes for the future.

We now come to the origin of the present war (1876). It appears that an Indian inspector, E.C. Watkins, under date of Nov 9th, 1875, made complaint to the Indian Bureau that Sitting Bull and other Indians with him, residing in the unceded territory, were engaged in making war upon friendly Indians and the white settlers of Montana. He recommended that "a force of one thousand men should be sent to compel them to submit to the Government." The Secretary of the Interior referred this letter to the Secretary of War for consideration and action.

December 15th, 1875, orders were given to General Sheridan to have the recommendations carried out; it would seem that in the early part of the winter of 1875-76, many Indians from the different Agencies went out with the consent of their agents to hunt Buffalo in the unceded country. They had the right to do this under the treaty. There was more reason for them to go at this time because there was an insufficient supply of provisions at the Agencies.

December 6, 1875, the Commissioner of Indian Affairs sent instructions to the several Agents to notify the Indians in the unceded territory to come to the Agencies before the 31st of January, 1876, or they would be regarded as hostile. The runner sent out by Agent Bingham to notify the Indians to return to the Agency, was not able to return himself until February 11th 1876. He brought back word that; "The Indians received the invitation and warning in good spirit and without any exhibition of ill feeling." They answered that, "They were engaged in hunting Buffalo and could not accept the invitation at present, but would return to the agency early in the Spring."

February 7th, 1876, authority was received by General Sheridan to commence operations against Hostile Sioux, who, Watkins' report says, were . . . "a small band of thirty or forty lodges under Sitting Bull, and the bands of other chiefs and headmen under Crazy Horse, numbering about one hundred and twenty lodges." On the 8th of February, General Terry, who commanded the Department in which Sitting Bull was supposed to be, was directed to take such steps with the forces under his command as would carry out the wishes of the Interior Department and the orders of the General of the Army. And he was also informed that General Crook had received similar orders and would operate from the South in the directions of Powder, Tongue, Rosebud and Bighorn rivers where Crazy Horse and his allies frequented. General Crook, with a force of ten companies of Cavalry and two companies of Infantry, started on the First of March from Fort Fetterman. On the 17th of March the main portion of the expedition struck an Indian village under Crazy Horse on Powder river, destroying all the lodges, 105 in number, and the ammunition and stores it contained, killing some Indians as well as capturing a large herd of horses. The horses were however, soon retaken by the Indians.

The command suffered so much from the severity of the weather that it had to return to Fort Fetterman and the troops were redistributed to their various winter stations to protect them from the extreme cold. It has been claimed by the Indians that this band was on its way to the Agency. This is hard to vouch for, but it may be so. In the meantime, General Terry had projected an expedition against Sitting Bull's bands which it was believed were located on the Little Missouri River. But before the troops could be concentrated at Fort Lincoln the season became so inclement and the snow so deep that it was thought advisable to abandon the expedition until later in the season.

Early in the spring, Generals Terry and Crook made preparations to resume operations, General Crook with Fifteen Companies of Cavalry and Five Companies of Infantry besides a lot of friendly Indian scouts started from Fort Fetterman, May 22nd, and established his supply camp on Goose Creek, on the 8th of June.

It was at first the intentions of General Terry to send out the expedition from Fort Lincoln early in April, and under the command of General Custer, but the latter was called to Washington in March as a witness before a House Committee that was investigating charges against the ex Secretary of War, General Belknap. It may be in order to say that General Belknap was a strong personal friend of President Grant upon whose staff he had served when the latter was in command of the Army, and later had been his Secretary of War, resigning the office but a short time previous while under fire of a threatened investigation, but still retaining the confidence, support and friendship of his former chief. It has been stated that the enmity, if such it may be called, of President Grant toward General Custer was a large factor in the disastrous expedition of 1876. That the strained relations between the two did result in delaying the starting of the expedition from Fort Lincoln, thereby allowing the Indians more time to consolidate their forces is undoubtedly a fact, and that General Custer had been deeply humiliated in his own eyes and those of his brother officers, is equally true. So that when he started on the expedition he was stung to the quick. And it can easily be imagined by anyone who knew the man that, if given the slightest opportunity he would not hesitate to take the greatest of risks to redeem himself. As to whom was the most to blame we leave the readers to judge for themselves, giving a brief outline of the cause as portrayed by Frederick Whittaker, in his *Life of General George A. Custer*, published in 1876, and Colonel Robert P. Hughes in *The Campaign against the Sioux in 1876* from official sources, published in 1896. Colonel Hughes being in 1876 a member of General Terry's staff.

The reasons for the summoning of General Custer as a witness were as follows. "On one occasion, the Contractor at Fort Lincoln had turned him over a large quantity of grain, in sacks, which bore the Indian brand, and which he suspected had been stolen from the Indian Department. At the time this grain was issued to Custer he refused to accept it, and telegraphed to Department Headquarters on the subject, expressing his suspicions. In due time he received a positive order to take the grain. Unfortunately for Custer, his suspicions, were given to much publicity, and as a result, he was summoned to Washington as a possible witness, and before the Committee he stated that he believed that the order to accept the grain came down from the Secretary of War."[1] The House Committee, at his most urgent request discharged him from further attendance and he was about to leave home when he was summoned by the Senate Committee, to repeat the same story. Anxious to get back to his command which was fitting for the field, he sought the aid of the Secretary of War who promised to write to the Committee after the Cabinet meeting that day. While at the meeting, the Secretary mentioned his intention to the President who directed him not to write to the Committee but to substitute some Officer for Custer in command. When this came to the knowledge of Custer he saw the Committee in person and obtained their permission to leave.[2] Before doing so he called at the White House to see the President, sent in his card, and a little later a letter. After waiting nearly five hours he was informed that the President would not see him. He thereupon started for his post but was intercepted at Chicago by a telegram to General Sheridan from General Sherman ordering that General Custer be detained at that point, or St. Paul.[3] This order was afterwards modified allowing him to go to Fort Lincoln for duty but not to accompany the expedition.[4] Custer proceeded to St. Paul where as a last resort, he sought the interposition of General Terry who yielded to his pleas and wrote and sent the following dispatch, of which every word including what is signed as Custer's was his own composition.

1. Frederick Whittaker, *A Complete Life of Major General George A. Custer,* p. 549.
2. Ibid., p. 553.
3. Ibid., p. 13.
4. Robert P. Hughes, "The Campaign Against the Sioux," p. 13.

Headquarters Department of Dakota,
Saint Paul, Minn.
May 6th, 1876.

The Adjutant General,
Division of the Missouri, Chicago.

I forward the following: To His Excellency, the President. (Through Military Channels)

I have seen your order transmitted through the General of the Army directing that I be not permitted to accompany the expedition to move against the hostile Indians. As my entire regiment forms a part of the expedition and as I am the senior Officer of the regiment on duty in this Department I respectfully but most earnestly request that while not allowed to go in command of the expedition I may be permitted to serve with my regiment in the field. I appeal to you as a Soldier to spare me the humiliation of seeing my regiment march to meet the enemy and I not to share its dangers.

    (signed) G. A. Custer

In forwarding the above I wish to say, expressly, that I have no desire whatever to question the orders of the President or of my Military superiors. Whether Lieutenant Colonel Custer shall be permitted to accompany the column or not I shall go in command of it. I do not know the reasons upon which the orders were given rest, but if these reasons do not forbid it Lieutenant Colonel Custer's services would be very valuable with his regiment.

    (signed) Alfred H. Terry
    Command Department

This was forwarded as indicated through Terry's military superiors and was endorsed by Sheridan as follows;

Chicago, Illinois.
May 7th 1876
Brigadier General E. D. Townsend.
Washington, D.C.

The following dispatch from General Terry is respectfully forwarded. I am sorry Lieutenant Colonel Custer did not manifest as much interest in staying at his post to organize and get ready his regiment and the expedition as he does now to accompany it. On a previous occasion in eighteen sixty eight I asked executive clemency for Colonel Custer to enable him to accompany his regiment against the Indians, and I sincerely hope that if granted this time it may have sufficient effect to prevent him from again attempting to throw discredit upon his profession and his brother officers.[5]

(signed) P.H. Sheridan Lieutenant General.

The result is shown by the following dispatch from General Sherman:

"To General A. H. Terry, St. Paul, Minn.
Headquarters of the Army,
Washington May 8th, 1876.

General Sheridan's enclosing yours of yesterday touching General Custer's urgent request to go under your command with regiment has been submitted to the President, who sent me word that if you want General Custer along he withdraws his objections. Advise Custer to be prudent, not to take along any newspaper men, who always make mischief, and to abstain from personalities in the future.

(signed) W.T. Sherman
General."

5. Ed. note: Refers to Custer's court-martial for having been absent without leave in 1865. Custer had left his post to check on his wife, who, he thought, might have contracted cholera during an epidemic.

The result of Terry's intercession was made known to Custer by General Terry at his Headquarters on the morning of May 8th, and early the next morning General Terry, with his staff of nine officers, accompanied by General Custer took the train for Bismarck, from there to go to Fort Lincoln to join the mobilized troops.

Rare photo of Lonesome Charley Reynolds, a scout killed with Custer at the Little Bighorn. Here he is wearing a derby hat, with Chief Charlie Hogg, and Hogg's wife and child. Circa 1875.

CHAPTER II

Getting Under Way

On a long but not very wide plateau, bordered by the Missouri river on the east and the everlasting prairie on the west, and about one half mile below the cavalry barracks at Fort Lincoln lay the camps of the forthcoming expedition.

The troops which had been gathered together for a campaign against the so called hostile Indians were taken from Forts Lincoln, Rice, Totten and Wadsworth in Dakota, with a few men from Fort Snelling, Minnesota and three troops of the Seventh Cavalry that had been serving in the southern states. Some of the companies had been in the camp for several weeks, and those coming from the South, Troops G, H, and K had, just previous to their arrival, received a large number of recruits, fresh from civil life. The fighting part of the expedition was composed of the following: twelve Troops [the entire Regiment] of the Seventh Cavalry. Two Companies of the Seventh Infantry. 28 Officers and about 700 men. [C and G] One Company of the Sixth Infantry. 8 Officers and 135 men. [B] Two Gatling Guns, under command of Lieutenant Rowe of the 20th Infantry, two Officers and 32 men. Thirty-four Arikara Indian Scouts, 4 friendly Sioux Scouts, 2 Half-breeds, (Jackson brothers) 2 Interpreters, Isaiah Dorman, [Colored] and Frank Girard a half-breed. 2 Guides, Charley Reynolds and a man named Berendotte. Two of General Custer's relatives, Boston Custer, a brother, and "Autie" Reed, a nephew, accompanied the command in civilian official capacity.

The wagon train, which was a large and expensive one as it was necessary to transport an immense amount of forage and rations, consisted of 114 Six mule teams, 37 Two mule teams, and 35 pack mules, giving employment in various capacities to 179 men. the Expedition numbering in all about 1140 souls.

Everything being in readiness it was decided to start on the 17th of May, and at five o'clock in the morning of that day the *"General"* was sounded by the Trumpeter at Headquarters. This was the Army signal [bugle call] to take down the tents and prepare to move. In a moment and almost as by magic the little white city was leveled to the ground. A few moments more and the tents were packed and the company wagons were starting for their place in the train. Before seven o'clock the cavalry had mounted and was marching around the parade ground of the cavalry barracks passing in front of the officers quarters and affording the officers' wives and families their last review of the Seventh. The morning was raw and cold, and a heavy mist hung over the whole region round about. It gradually rose, however, as we passed Fort Lincoln, and when we reached the foot of the long ascent leading up to the prairie above, it was a very beautiful sight, that of the gradual fading out of the mist-bows and the rolling upward of the mist.

General Custer's wife, and his sister, Mrs. James Calhoun, accompanied us on the first day's march and they rode beside him at the head of the Regiment; the incidents of the beginning of our march and the impression they made on Mrs. Custer have been so vividly described in her book *Boots and Saddles*, that I take the liberty to make the following brief extract, believing that her story, will have especial interest.[1]

She says: "As we rode at the head of the column we were the first to enter the confines of the garrison. About the Indian quarters which we were obliged to pass, stood the squaws, the old men, and the children singing, or rather moaning a minor tune that has been uttered on the going out of Indian warriors since time immemorial. Some of the squaws crouched on the ground, too burdened with their trouble to hold up their heads. The Indian scouts themselves beat their drums and kept up their peculiar monotonous tune which is weird and melancholy beyond description. It is more of a

1. Ed. note: Taylor, while quoting from *Boots and Saddles*, does so selectively, as some passages were excluded or shortened from the original text.

lament or a dirge than an inspiration to activity. This intoning they kept up for miles along the road.

"After we had passed the Indian quarters we came near Laundress Row, and there my heart entirely failed me. The wives and children of the soldiers lined the road. Mothers, with streaming eyes held their little ones out at arms length for one last look at the departing father. Unfettered by conventional restrictions, and indifferent to the opinion of others, the grief of these women was audible, and was accompanied by desponding gestures, dictated by their bursting hearts and expressions of their abandoned grief. It was a relief to escape from them and enter the garrison, and yet when our band struck up *The Girl I left Behind Me,*" the most despairing hour seemed to have come. All the sad faced wives of the officers who had forced themselves to their doors to try and wave a courageous farewell and smile bravely to keep the ones they loved from knowing the anguish of their breaking hearts gave up the struggle at the sound of the music. The first notes made them disappear to fight out alone their trouble, and to place their hands in that of their Heavenly Father, who, at such supreme hour, was their never failing solace.

Rare portrait of Elizabeth B. Custer, possibly an unpublished image. Circa 1865.

"From the hour of breaking camp, before the sun was up, a mist had enveloped everything. Soon the bright sun began to penetrate this veil and dispel the haze, and a scene of wonder and beauty appeared, The cavalry and infantry in the order named, the scouts, pack mules, and artillery. All behind the long line of white covered wagons, made a column altogether some two miles in length. As the sun broke through the mist a mirage appeared, which took up about half of the line of cavalry, and thenceforth for a little distance it marched equally plain to the sight on the earth and in the sky.

"The future of the heroic band, whose days were even then numbered, seemed to be revealed, and already there seemed a premonition in the supernatural translation as their forms were reflected from the opaque mist of the early dawn."[2]

2. *Boots and Saddles*, p. 217.

After ascending the heights back of the cavalry barracks, and passing close by the Fort on the hill, which was originally Fort McKean, but was later renamed Fort Abraham Lincoln, and garrisoned by an infantry command, the line of march was taken up almost due west for Heart River. The route was over a rolling prairie, and at half past one in the afternoon, after a march of about 13 miles we encamped on Heart River. This was the first water we had seen since leaving Fort Lincoln, a not at all uncommon incident of our campaigning. Here, soon after our camp was established, the military part of the command received their pay for the past two months from the Paymaster who has come out with us for that sole purpose, and who with a small escort returned to Fort Lincoln the next morning accompanied by Mrs. Custer and Mrs. Calhoun.[3]

Our Indian Scouts, who were mostly of the Arikara tribe and generally called "Rees", furnished much amusement and interest for many of the command. They were of medium size and quite dark, and had at all times a dirty appearance, and one officer said. "They looked much like antiquated negro washerwomen." They paid but little attention to their personal appearance, and but slight attempts at ornamentation of any kind. Their hatred and fear of the Sioux with whom their tribe had long been at enmity, was most genuine and thorough. Their best man was "Bloody Knife", who was half Sioux and half "Ree". He was General Custer's favorite scout, and a fighter to the last breath.

The next morning, [18th] the command resumed the march, crossing Heart River which was at this point about 30 yards wide, and 3 feet deep, but little progress was made this day, however, nor for several days after. The moving of a large wagon train over a trailless and unknown country was a slow and discouraging task. At this time there was not a ranch between Bismarck, Dakota Territory and Bozeman, Montana. Today the N.P.R.R. practically follows our line of march most of the way to the Yellowstone, and thriving towns and settlements dot the site of some of our camping places and the trail we made was in evidence for many years after. Most of our way to the Little Missouri a feasible route had to be located to accommodate the

3. Ed. note: The civilian teamsters and Indian scouts did not receive their pay at the same time as the troops.

Wagon train. There were many coulees the banks of which had to be cut away to make a passage for the heavy laden wagons. Narrow streams had to be bridged, some of them were very tortuous and in one case we made ten crossings in eight miles. At the end of four days we had just reached the Little Muddy, where we went into camp, some 46 miles from Fort Lincoln. Here some scouts were sent back with letters and dispatches, starting after dark so as to avoid being seen by any watching party of hostiles, no signs of which had as yet been seen although they had been reported as having camped on the Little Missouri during the preceding winter.

Entering the Badlands we went into the Little Missouri, May 29th, not far from the present village of Medora. The Badlands, as seen from a distance, present a very striking and picturesque appearance. "Like a ruined world it seemed burnt, upturned and scarred by fire". This effect is heightened by occasional patches of red and yellow clay which glisten in the sunlight like beacon fires. On a near approach one finds deep and tortuous ravines flanked by almost perpendicular bluffs. In addition, there are numerous solitary formations, usually conical in shape and running from five to fifty feet in height, some of them having layers or bands very distinctly marked as with a brush, the shades running through black, red, yellow, blue, and gray to pure white. General Sully's first sight of the Badlands, in 1864, brought out the exclamation, "Gentlemen, it looks like the bottom of Hell, with the fires out."

The location was not altogether unknown to many of us for it was this point that we crossed the river in 1873 while engaged in General Stanley's Yellowstone Expedition.[4] The next day was spent in camp by the main part of the command while General Custer with four troops of our regiment made a scouting march of some 25 miles up the Little Missouri, to ascertain if there were any Indians in that neighborhood as had been reported. He found no recent signs and returned before dark after a long and tiresome ride of fifty miles.

The next day, passing a little south of the "Sentinel Buttes," we made a short march and again went into camp where a heavy snow storm during the night, compelled us to remain for the next two days.

4. The Yellowstone Expedition was a government-sponsored undertaking to survey the region west of the Missouri River for the future extension of the Northern Pacific Railroad westward into Montana.

Pine trees, at our feet was the Bad Land formation, with its deep, yawning chasms and its various colored earth, fash-ioned into weird and fantastic shapes by the rains and floods. Leading up from these were long ravines with their thick growth of timber, the dark green hue of which formed a strong and beautiful contrast to the softer and lighter shade of the grass covered hills. To the right there stretched out a rolling country backed in the distance by the Yellowstone bluffs. Continuing our march we reached the Powder River about 7 oclock P.M. and went into camp, about 20 miles from its junction with the Yellowstone, having made a march of 32 miles, the longest of the trip, so far. The next day, June 10th Major Reno with six Troops of the Regiment, a Gatling gun, and a few scouts, left camp in the afternoon for a scout up the Powder River, taking rations for ten days. His orders were to ascend the Powder to its forks, thence across to Mizpah Creek, down that Creek for a distance and then over to Tongue River and down to its mouth. On the 11th the remainder of the command moved down to the Yellowstone where a Supply Camp was established, the wagon train being left there with the Infantry Companies under Major Moore as a guard. The total distance marched up to this time

*   *   *

Starting again on the morning of June 3rd we made but a few miles when we met some scouts sent out by General Gibbon who was then on the Yellowstone not far from the mouth of Powder River. A march of 25 miles brought us to Beaver Creek, a tributary to the Little Missouri. The Creek at this point was about 30 feet wide and from one to six feet deep, the water being very cool and clear. Turning southward we followed Beaver Creek crossing several tributaries until we came to a crossing place over the main stream. From there the route led to O'Fallon's Creek, a tributary of the Yellowstone. This march was a most difficult one for the wagon train to follow as none of our guides were at all familiar with this section of the country, but General Custer had a great faculty for finding a roadway and believing in his ability took "D" Troop and the scouts and started ahead. The country was very rough and uninteresting for a portion of the way and rendered more dreary by a cold drizzling rain, but after ascending the divide the sight was one long to be remembered. To our left was Powder River ridge with its fringe of pine trees. At our feet was the Badland formation, with its deep, yawning chasms and its various colored earths, fashioned into weird and fantastic shapes by the rains and floods. Leading up from these were long ravines with their thick growth of timber, the dark green hue of which formed a strong and beautiful contrast to the softer and lighter shade of the grass-covered hills.

To the right there stretched out a rolling country backed in the distance by the Yellowstone bluffs. Continuing our march we reached the Powder River about 7 o'clock p.m. and went into camp about 20 miles from its junction with the Yellowstone, having made a march of 32 miles, the longest of the trip so far. The next day, June 10th, Major Reno with six Troops of the Regiment, a Gatling gun, and a few scouts, left camp in the afternoon for a scout up the Powder River, taking rations for ten days. His orders were to ascend the Powder to its forks, thence across to Mizpah Creek, down that Creek for a distance and then over to the Tongue River and down to its mouth. On the 11th the remainder of the command moved down to the Yellowstone where a supply camp was established, the wagon train being left there with the Infantry companies under Major Moore as a guard. The total distance marched up to this time was, in round numbers, 320 miles.

We remained here until the 15th of June when General Custer with the remaining six Troops of the Regiment, one Gatling gun, the scouts and a train of pack mules marched up the south side of the Yellowstone bound for the Tongue River; General Terry and his Staff proceeding up the Yellowstone on the Steamer [Far West] for the same point, where it was expected to meet General Gibbon's command, which had been in the field since the 17th of March.

We reached the mouth of the Tongue River early on the 17th, and encamped on the site of a large Indian village. This had evidently been a favorite camping place for the Indians for nearby were numerous scaffold graves. Some bodies were found lashed in trees.[5] Some of the graves were dispoiled by the soldiers. One body, that gave forth a very offensive odor, was taken down and pitched into the river. Miles City, Montana was first built on the site of this camp.

On our march to this point we had passed the sites of several Indian villages and in one of them, General Custer, who was riding at the head of the column, suddenly came upon a human skull lying under the remains of an extinct fire, and stopping to examine it he found lying near by a portion of a U.S. Cavalryman's uniform as evidenced by the buttons on the overcoat being stamped with the letter "C" and the remains of the dresscoat having the yellow cord of the Cavalry running through it. The skull was weather beaten and had evidently been there several months.

All the circumstances went to show that the skull was that of some poor mortal who had been a prisoner in the hands of savages, and who doubtless had been tortured to death, probably burned.[6] ". . . and the events so soon to come, were casting their shadows before."

5. Ed. note: Many of the Plains tribes, especially the Sioux, abhorred the concept of placing their dead in the ground. According to Sioux belief, the human soul would be trapped in the earth, unable to escape to the Spirit World. This belief continued into the twentieth century.
6. Paraphrased by Taylor from *Boots and Saddles*, p. 274.

CHAPTER III

Finding the Trail

About sunset on the 19th a scout bearing a dispatch from Major Reno reached General Terry, in which Major Reno stated that he had scouted to the Rose-bud and beyond and had found a heavy Indian trail, estimated to have been made by about 350 lodges,[1] which he had followed until satisfied that it led to the Little Bighorn when he left it and descended the Rosebud to its mouth.

Word was at once sent back to Major Reno to remain where he was and await the coming of General Custer with the remainder of the Regiment. Starting out the next day, [June 21] we reached the mouth of the Rosebud about noon, and right glad were we to meet our comrades again. About four miles below us, on the other side of the Yellowstone, were the Montana troops under General Gibbon. General Terry had come up on the Steamer *Far West* and a conference was at once held by Generals Terry, Gibbon and Custer. A plan of campaign was agreed upon, which it was hoped, might be productive of the desired results; the capture of or infliction of a smashing defeat on the hostile Indians.

It was believed, from the observations of General Gibbon's command which had been scouting up and down the Yellowstone, and from the report that Major Reno had just brought in, that the Indians whom we were seeking would be found within a short distance of the mouth of the Little Bighorn.

"In his official orders General Custer was given a certain latitude of action. He was also given certain specific directions which to my knowledge were not carried out. Whether he was justified in ignoring them, under the circumstances, it is not for me to say; only this, that for his sake I wish he had not."

1. Ed. note: In many instances, a lodge was more than a single family unit; it could include extended-family members and relatives who lived together for mutual support and protection.

To this point General Gibbon's command was to proceed at once, General Terry and Staff going also, but on the *Far West*. General Custer, with the Seventh Cavalry and scouts, was to take up the trail Major Reno had found and follow it, to some conclusion. General Terry's instructions to Custer were communicated to him in writing. The question as to whether General Custer fully obeyed these instructions has been extensively debated by competent officers of the Army, some of whom were present on the Expedition, but without settling the matter except perhaps to the side taken. It would therefore be unbecoming for one who took a very subordinate part to pronounce a judgment.

In his official orders General Custer was given a certain latitude of action. He was also given certain specific directions which to my knowledge were not carried out. Whether he was justified in ignoring them, under the circumstances, it is not for me to say; only this, that for his sake I wish he had not.

* * *

The next day, June 22nd, the Regiment taking a pack train with 15 days rations, broke camp at twelve o'clock and after passing in review of General Terry, Gibbon, and Custer, started up the Valley of the Rosebud. It seems a fitting place to introduce two extracts from the last letter written to his wife by General Custer, extracts which she prints in her most interesting Book entitled, *Boots and Saddles*. The letter is dated "Mouth of the Rosebud, June 22nd."

> The scouting party has returned, they saw the trail and deserted camp of a village of 380 lodges, the trail was about one week old. The scouts reported that they could have overtaken the village in one day and a half. I am now going to take up the trail where the scouting party turned back, I fear their failure to follow up the Indians has imperiled our plans by giving the village an intimation of our presence. Think of the valuable time lost, but I feel hopeful of accomplishing great results.——I now have some Crow scouts

with me as they are familiar with the country. They are magnificent look-ing men, so much handsomer and Indian like than any we have ever seen, and so jolly and sportive; nothing of the gloomy, silent redman about them. They have formally given themselves to me, after the usual talk. In their speech they said they had heard that I never abandoned a trail; that when my food gave out I ate mule. That was the kind of a man they wanted to fight under. They were willing to eat mule too.

I am going to send six Ree scouts to the Powder river with the mail, from there it will go with other scouts to Fort Buford.[2]

Leaving our camp on the Yellowstone, a short distance below the mouth of the Rosebud we marched up to the latter stream where we crossed to the west side and continued up its valley. Owing to delays incidental to the break-ing in of a new pack train, and our late start, the command moved but 12 miles and went into camp on the left bank of the Rosebud. Here we were informed that trumpet calls would be discontinued, and the men would be aroused at 3 a.m. by the stable guard and the command would move at 5 a.m.

At the appointed time we started out on the 23rd, crossing and recrossing the stream many times during the day, striking the trail made by Major Reno a few days before and soon coming on many evidences of a large body of Indians having been camped along the river. We made camp about 4:30. p.m. having rode some 30 miles.

June 24th, we started as usual at 5 a.m. Soon after we had got under way the Crow scouts returned to the column and reported fresh signs of Indians at the forks of the Rosebud, and on the march we passed through sev-eral lately abandoned camping places. The trail was growing fresher every mile and the whole valley was scratched up by trailing lodgepoles. Our inter-est grew in proportion as the trail freshened and there was much speculation in the ranks as to how soon we should overtake the apparently fleeing enemy. But the hour had not come, though it was fast drawing near, and we rode on and on until about 7 o'clock p.m., when we went into camp, having marched about 28 miles.

2. *Boots and Saddles*, pp. 274–75.

The march during the day had been a rather tiresome one for
we had halted many times, in order to give the scouts an opp-
-ertunity to thoroughly examine the valley ahead of us,
After our horses had been fed and rubbed down, and our
simple meal of Coffee and Hardtack disposed of the men
spreading their peice of shelter tent and blanket on the
ground lay down for a much needed rest.
The spot that had been chosen for our Bivouac was one of
the most beautiful that we had met with, on our right
rose a high, and for a short distance almost perpendicular
bluff, between which and the river, a clear, cool, running
stream, was a level grassy plautau some two hundred
yards wide, over which was scattered in great profusion
masses of wild Rose bushes in full bloom, with here and
there a tree to add to the Park like effect. It was easy to see
why the river was given its name, fringed as it was with low
willows and fragrent Rosebushes, it was such a place for a camp
that Custer was in the habit of selecting when possible
one of great natures beauty, in this case it seemed so
very fitting that what was to prove to be the "last
camp" for so many should be such a beautiful place.
I have often wished since that time that the spot might
be located and a photograph obtained, but to continue

my Troop, it, was quite near to Custers headquarters, a single
A tent, before which he sat for a long time alone and apparently in deep thought, I was lying on my side, facing him,
and was it my fancy, or the gathering twilight that made
his face take on an expression of sadness that was new to me.
was it because his thoughts were far away, back to Fort Lincoln
where he had left a most beloved wife, and was his heart
filled with a premonition of what was to happen on the
morrow, His reverie however was soon broken by the gathering
of a number of Officers at his tent for certain instructions.
as the council broke up, a small group of the younger
Officers stopped near the bivouac of one of their number and soon
the words of "Annie Laurie", with a slow, sad cadence came
to my ears, followed shortly by "Little Footsteps, Soft and Gentle,"
and then, "The Good By at the Door," ending with the "Doxology"
Praise God from whom all Blessings flow," a rather strange
song for Cavalrymen to sing on an Indian trail, was it
not something in the nature of a prayer comeing from
the hearts of those young Officers, several of them but a short
time from West Point, and may it not have been born of
an unconscious premonition of the sad fate that so soon
awaited many of them, but as the last words died away, as
if to throw off their gloomy feelings they added

The march during the day had been a rather tiresome one for we had halted many times in order to give the scouts an opportunity to thoroughly examine the valley ahead of us. After our horses had been fed and rubbed down, and our simple meal of coffee and hardtack disposed of the men, spreading their piece of shelter tent and blanket on the ground, lay down for a much needed rest.

The spot that had been chosen for our bivouac was one of the most beautiful that we had met with. On our right rose a high, and for a short distance almost perpendicular bluff, between which and the river, a clear, cool, running stream, was a level grassy plateau some two hundred yards wide. Over which was scattered in great profusion masses of wild rosebushes in full bloom, with here and there a tree to add to the park like effect. It was easy to see why the river was given its name, fringed as it was with low willows and fragrant rosebushes, it was such a place for a camp that Custer was in the habit of selecting when possible one of great natural beauty. In this case it seemed so very fitting that what was to prove to be the "last camp" for so many should be such a beautiful place. I have often wished since that time that the spot might be located and a photograph obtained.

But to continue, my Troop [A] was quite near to Custer's headquarters, a single "A" tent, before which he sat for a long time alone and apparently in deep thought. I was lying on my side, facing him, and was it my fancy, or the gathering twilight that made his face take on an expression of sadness that was new to me. Was it because his thoughts were far away, back to Fort Lincoln where he had left a most beloved wife, and was his heart filled with a premonition of what was to happen on the morrow? His reverie however was soon broken by the gathering of a number of officers at his tent for certain instructions. As the council broke up a small group of the younger officers stopped near the bivouac of one of their number and soon the words of *"Annie Laurie"*, with a slow sad cadence came to my ears, followed shortly by *"Little Footsteps, Soft and Gentle"*, and then, *"The Good Bye at the Door"*, ending with the *"Doxology: Praise God From Whom all Blessings Flow"*, a rather strange song for Cavalrymen to sing on an Indian trail. Was it not something in the nature of a prayer coming from the hearts of those young officers, several of them but a short time from West Point? May it not have been born of an unconscious premonition of the sad fate that so soon awaited many of them? But as the last words died away, as if to throw off their gloomy feelings they added *"For He's a Jolly Goodfellow, That Nobody Can Deny;"* rather irreverent it seemed to me at the time, but then reverence, of a religious nature, is not altogether a soldier's characteristic. A few "good nights" and they sought their rest. An unusual quietness settled over the camp, broken only by the stamping of a horse or the note of some night bird.

As we lay there in that lovely and quiet bivouac, in a section of "the Indian's Paradise land," where we had never been before, how little could anyone think that a fierce battle had taken place only a short distance above us and just a week before when Crazy Horse stopped the advance of General Crook with a much larger force than our own. Nor could the strongest imagination foresee that in a little over a month the same hostiles we were then pursuing, flushed with another and far greater victory, could again be camping here on this beautiful stream, only to be hurried away by the close approach of General Terry from the north over the very trail we had just made and the second appearance of General Crook coming down the river from the south. How could we dream that the command now in camp was to encircle a large section of the country and come back to the same spot after the same hostile force we were now pursuing, or that, within a few miles of where we lay, the brave and unconquered "Lame Deer" would soon give up his life for the right to live and hunt along this rose-bordered stream, and his name, to the agency, set apart in after years, to his tribesmen.

*   *   *

Our rest here proved to be but for a few hours only, for about ten o'clock we were awakened and ordered to saddle up for a night march. We were soon in the saddle and, still following the Rosebud, marched some ten miles or more ascending the north fork of the river up the divide separating the Rosebud from the Little Bighorn.

Mr. Finerty, in his *War-Path and Bivouac*, has so very graphically and truthfully described a night march along this same river, and only a few weeks later. I hope to be excused for using a portion of his description, which will apply in every particular to our own march on the night of June 24th/25th. He says:

> The moon did not rise for some hours and the night was dark as Erebus, intense silence pervaded the line of march and not a sound was heard but the solemn tramp of the cavalry column, advancing through the gloom, and the occasional bray of some mule in the pack train. A night march in the Indian wilderness of the North is one of the most impressive incidents of war, it is weird, outre and inspiring, the vastness of untamed nature is around you and its influence is insensibly felt. You are on the track of a mysterious enemy, the country over which you are marching is to you an unread chapter. You see something like a black shadow moving in advance. You are conscious that men and animals are moving within a few paces, and yet you cannot define any particular object, not even your horse's head. But you hear the steady, perpetual "tramp-tramp-tramp" of the iron hoofed cavalry, broken by an occasional stumble and the half smothered imprecation of an irate trooper; the jingle of carbines and sling-belts, and the snorting of the horses as they grope their way through the eternal dust, which the rider can feel in his throat. Once in a while a match, struck by a soldier to light his pipe, would flash in the gloom, like a huge firefly, and darkness would again assert itself.[3]

We halted somewhere about 2 a.m. awaiting news from the scouts who had been sent ahead to locate, if possible, the camp of the Indians. Saddles were removed and many of the men availed themselves of the chance for a nap. After daylight came some coffee was made but the water was very poor and it was hard to drink it. Those who did not care to sleep sat around in little groups discussing the prospects of a fight and pulling away at the ever present pipe.

3. John F. Finerty, *War-Path and Bivouac*, p. 158. Ed. note: In this passage Taylor borrows liberally from Finerty without quoting him exactly.

General Custer who had gone on ahead to the point on the divide from whence the scouts had seen the smoke rising from the Indian village and the pony herds grazing in the valley near it, some twelve or fifteen miles away, had returned, and a little before eight o'clock came riding bareback, and I think also bareheaded, around to the several troops giving the officers the information that the Indians had been located, and saying that the command would move at once. The men began to saddle up and we were soon in motion travelling up the divide between the Rosebud and Little Bighorn rivers. We did not stop until about 10:30 a.m. when we came to a halt in a ravine, some four or five miles perhaps from the summit of the divide. Here we were ordered to keep concealed, and to preserve quiet. Captain Godfrey

Image of Custer wearing undress uniform and campaign hat, by Mathew Brady. Signed: *Custer.* Circa 1865.

says, "It was Custer's declared intention not to attack until the next morning". But in the meantime our presence having been discovered, so the scouts and the others reported, "it was necessary to act at once,"[4] and we started off again crossing the divide a little before noon.

Soon afterwards the Regiment was divided into Battalions, the advance Battalion under Major Reno consisted of troop M, Captain French, troop A, Captain Moylan and Lieutenant DeRudio, troop G. Lieutenants McIntosh and Wallace; the Indian scouts, about 30 in number under Lieutenants Varnum and Hare, with two interpreters Isaiah Dorman, colored, and Frank Girard, half-breed. There were also three white scouts; Charley Reynolds, George Herendeen and a man named Berendotte; two medical officers, Dr. De Wolf and Dr. Porter. The exact number of the Battalion is not known, but it was probably a little less than 150 all told.

Captain Benteen's Battalion, consisting of troops D, H, and K, about 125 men, moved off to our left front, while General Custer with troops C, E, F, J, and L, were on our right. the pack-trains, with Captain McDougal and B troop as escort bringing up the rear.

4. W. A. Graham, *The Custer Myth*. Edward S. Godfrey's narrative appears on p. 138.

CHAPTER IV

Reno's Attack

Major Reno's Battalion, following the Indian trail, marched down a valley through which ran what has since been called Benteen's, or Sundance Creek. This creek flowed into the Little Bighorn river, when there was any water in it, but at this time it was dry. On our way we passed a funeral tepee, which contained the body of a warrior. The tepee had been set on fire by some of our Indian scouts. Afterwards it was learned that the dead warrior was a brother of Circling Bear [Old She Bear][1] and had been killed in the battle with Crook on the Rosebud, June 17th, eight days before. It has been stated that "a few Indians were seen near here," and that they kept far enough in advance to be out of danger. As to that I can not say, personally I did not see any of them. When, within a short distance of the river, Reno received an order that caused us to increase our speed and we soon came to the Little Bighorn, a stream some fifty to seventy feet wide, and from two to four feet deep of clear, icy cold water.

> "The Death Angel was very near. Was he putting his seal on those who inside of an hour would be lying on the prairie or in the woods, dead, stripped and gashed almost beyond recognition?"

Into it our horses plunged without any urging, their thirst was great and also their riders. While waiting for them to drink I took off my hat and, shaping the brim into a scoop, leaned over, filled it and drank the last drop of water I was to have for over twenty-four long hours. The horses having been watered, we rode out of the river and through the underbrush and then a few yards on the prairie, where we dismounted and tightened our saddle girths,

---

1. David Humphries Miller, *Custer's Fall*, p. 75.

Major Marcus Reno, the author's commanding officer.

2. Ed. note: Taylor's veiled and offhand inference that Reno may have been intoxicated is revealing of Taylor's opinion of Reno. During the Reno court of inquiry, testimony was given that appeared to vindicate Reno on the charge of drunkenness, though he did admit to having had several drinks. See Robert M. Utley, ed., *The Reno Court of Inquiry*, pp. 225, 372, 381.

and in about ten minutes were heading down a long but rather narrow valley.

On our right was the heavily wooded and very irregular course of the river, flanked by high bluffs. On our left were low foothills near which we could see a part of the pony herds, and as we came nearer, could distinguish mounted men riding in every direction, some in circles, others passing back and forth. They were gathering up their ponies and also making signals. We were then at a fast walk. Soon the command was given to "trot". Then as little puffs of smoke were seen and the "Ping" of bullets spoke out plainly, we were ordered to charge.

Some of the men began to cheer in reply to the Indians war whoops when Major Reno shouted out, "Stop that noise," and once more there came the command, "Charge!" "Charrrge!" was the way it sounded to me, and it came in such a tone that I turned my head and glanced backward.

The Major and Lieutenant Hodgson were riding side by side a short distance in the rear of my Company. As I looked back Major Reno was just taking a bottle from his lips. He then passed it to Lieutenant Hodgson. It appeared to be a quart flask, and about one half or two thirds full of an amber colored liquid. There was nothing strange about this, and yet the circumstances remained indelibly fixed in my memory. I turned my head to the front as there were other things to claim my attention. What that flask contained, and effect its contents has, is not for me to say, but I have ever since had a very decided belief.[2]

In the "Count Off" that morning I was number four, hence when the Troops were dismounted, to fight on foot, every fourth man had three led horses to care for. The position at that time was not to me a desirable one as I wanted to be in the fight, and I had tried in vain to exchange places with my number three man. I have since thought that it was very fortunate perhaps that I did not succeed, for this man, Cornelius Crowley by name, had lately been showing signs of mental eccentricity, or in other words seemed to be losing his mind and the engagement brought matters to a climax in his case. And thereafter he was, so far as possible, kept in charge by the Stable Guard. Had we exchanged places and he had three other excited horses to care for it is a question if he would have been found when we returned to the woods for our horses.

But to resume, the river as I have already said, was a very tortuous one, and at this point it came well out into the prairie, made a sharp turn and then went back to the bluffs. It was lined on both sides by tall cottonwood trees, and its banks, thick with underbrush so that it shut off the view of the nearest part of the Indian Village which we were fast approaching. Over sage and bullberry bushes, over prickly pears and through a prairie dog village without a thought we rode. A glance along the line shows a lot of set, determined faces, some of them a little pale perhaps, but not altogether with fear. The Death Angel was very near. Was he putting his seal on those who inside of an hour would be lying on the prairie or in the woods, dead, stripped and gashed almost beyond recognition? Be that as it may, there was no flinching on the part of anyone. To most of us it was our first real battle at close range. Our baptism of fire, a new and strange experience, to sit up as a human target, to be shot at and not to return the fire, was a little trying, but our turn was at hand.

"Halt!", came the sharp, quick order, "Prepare to fight on foot", follows at once. Every fourth man from the right remained in his saddle, the others dismounted and tying their horse together, handed the bridle reins to the number four man and sprang forward to their places in the skirmish line. When I look back and think of the sublime audacity of one hundred and fifty Cavalrymen charging with a cheer down on an Indian village that contained at least, twenty-five hundred Sioux warriors, and when within close range, dismounting to fight on foot leaving one fourth of their number to hold the horses, it does seems indeed like madness, one hundred fifty men to charge on a village of 1800 lodges.

The led horses, under the charge of Lieutenant Hare, were then

---

taken into the woods for greater safety, keeping slightly in rear of the skirmish line. Just how long we remained there I can not say, but I shall never believe that it was over fifteen or twenty minutes at the most. I did not see Major Reno while in the woods nor do I recall hearing any commands as to what we should do. Noise there was aplenty and a few shots went whistling through the underbrush.

All at once the skirmishers came rushing into the woods seeking their horses which they could not locate at first owing to the underbrush, and a slight change of position. Then I heard someone say, "We must get our of here, quick!"

Number one and two of my set of four saw me and at once took their horses, leaving me with Con Crowley's horse, and wondering where he was. I soon espied him at a little distance rushing around and shouting "Where's my horse, Where's my horse?" I yelled at him, perhaps not politely, but effectively, for he hastened toward me. I threw him the bridle-rein and turned my horse in the direction I had seen the men going. All was in the greatest confusion and I dismounted twice and mounted again, all in a few moments, but why, I do not know, unless it was because I saw the others do it and thought they had orders to.

Before I had gone many yards, I looked to my left and rear and saw quite a number of mounted Indians rushing through the woods in the same general direction we were going, as if they were trying to cut off the men who had preceded me. They were so near that my first thought was that they were some of our Indian scouts, but a second look undeceived me. For these Indians were mostly stripped to their fighting costume, a breech-clout at one end, a feather at the other, a whip hanging from their wrist and a gun in their hand. There was one exception however, a sturdy looking chap who was the nearest of all. He wore a magnificent war bonnet of great long feathers encircling his head and hanging down his back, the end trailing along the side of his pony. I did want to take a shot at him but the trees were close together, and I was not a very good marksman.[3] Besides, my comrades seemed bent on getting out of there as soon as possible. So I let him live; I have often won-

3. Ed. note: The army supplied the forts with such limited amounts of ammunition that many new recruits had little, if any, training in marksmanship.

Over Sage and Bullberry bushes, over Prickly Pears and through
a Prairie Dog village without a thought we rode, a glance along
the line shows a lot of set, determined faces, some of them
a little pale perhaps, but not altogether with fear, The Death
Angle was very near, ? was he putting his seal on those who
inside of an hour would be lying on the prairie or in the woods,
dead, stripped and gashed almost beyond recognition. Be that
as it may, there was no flinching on the part of any one,
To most of us it was our first real battle, at close
range, our Baptisism of fire, a new and strange experience, to
sit up as a human target, to be shot at and not to return
the fire was a little trying, But our turn was at hand
"Halt," came the sharp, quick order, "Prepare to fight on foot,"
follows at once, every fourth man from the right remained in
his saddle, the others dismounted and tying their horses together,
handed the bridle reins to the number four man and
sprang forward to their places in the skirmish line.
When I look back and think of the sublime audacity
of one hundred and fifty, Cavalrymen charging with a cheer
down on an Indian Village that contained at least, twenty-five
hundred Sioux warriors, and when within close range,
dismounting to fight on foot leaving one fourth of their number
to hold the horses, it does seems indeed like madness one hundred and fifteen men
to charge on a village of 1800 lodges

best horsemen, the most cruel and fiercest fighters in all our
country, or any other. They had passed around our left and
prevented our return to the ford where we had first crossed the
river and now the nearest of them from the opposite side of
their ponies were pouring in a most terrific fire.
On my left was a line of my comrades headed due east
toward the bluffs which were one half to three-fourths of a mile
away and at the base of which flowed the river its banks at
at this point being high and precipitous and more or less
fringed with a thick growth of under brush.
The situation was most serious, it was so sudden and incomp-
-rehensible, a few moments before we were "driving the Indians
with great ease." (Renos Report) now, we were the driven, but there was
no time for speculation, Each man ahead of me had his right
arm extended fireing his revolver at a parallel line of yelling
Indians and I at once followed suit. Talk about the "thin red
line of the English," here was a thick red line, of Sioux and
growing thicker every moment. Out of the clouds of dust, anxious
to be in at the death, came hundreds of others shouting and raceing
toward the Soldiers most of whom were seeing their first battle and
many of whom I was one, had never fired a shot from a horses back
as before stated my right Stirrup was useless and in consequence my seat
was not very secure, nor my aim as accurate as it might have been, so I can

dered since then if that fellow was not one of the, "Big Chiefs", Gall, or Black-Moon. However, I continued on my way. The underbrush was very thick and in breaking my way through it my right stirrup was caught and the strap that attached it to the saddle was torn nearly off, so much so that the stirrup was useless and I had to be very careful of my balance. In far less time than it has taken to write this, I emerged from the woods, climbed up a little bank and came out on the prairie a short distance from where we first entered the woods.

The sight that greeted my eyes was certainly very discouraging. Not over two hundred yards away was a large and constantly increasing number of Indian warriors coming toward us as fast as their ponies could travel, a whooping, howling mass of the best horsemen, the most cruel and fiercest fighters in all our country, or any other. They had passed around our left and prevented our return to the ford where we had first crossed the river and now the nearest of them from the opposite side of their ponies were pouring in a most terrific fire.

On my left was a line of comrades headed due east toward the bluffs, which were one half to three-fourths of a mile away and at the base of which flowed the river, its banks at this point being high and precipitous and more or less fringed with a thick growth of underbrush.

The situation was most serious, it was so sudden and incomprehensible. A few moments before, we were "driving the Indians with great ease." [Reno's Report.] Now we were the driven, but there was no time for speculation. Each man ahead of me had his right arm extended firing his revolver at a parallel line of yelling Indians and I at once followed suit. Talk about the "Thin Red Line" of the English. Here was a thick Red line of Sioux and growing thicker every moment. Out of the clouds of dust, anxious to be in at the death, came hundreds of others, shouting and racing toward the soldiers, most of whom were seeing their first battle, and many, of whom I was one, had never fired a shot from a horse's back.

As before stated, my right stirrup was useless and in consequence my seat was not very secure, nor my aim as accurate as it might have been, so I can not say that I did much execution, but I tried to, firing at an Indian directly opposite who I thought was paying special attention to myself. At such a time many thoughts will pass through one's mind with great rapidity. The chances of being wounded or captured were many. One's fate in such a case was easy to imagine, so I reserved one of the six bullets that my revolver contained for the "last resort," myself, but I was not destined to use it in that manner.

A great part of our way lay through a prairie-dog village and the numerous holes and mounds made it very unpleasant riding at our rapid gait, for you could not tell what moment your horse might put his foot in a hole and throw you to the ground. A few moments of such riding brought me to what had been, ages ago, the bed of the river. It was some three or four feet lower with a rather abrupt bank down which with a little urging my horse jumped. And as he did so, to steady myself, I reached for the pommel of my saddle with my right hand which still held my revolver. As I did this my revolver fell to the ground, the Indians were crowding in closer, for as they afterwards said "they thought to drive us all into the river and drown us," and I deemed it very unwise to dismount and look for it in the tall grass and weeds. So I hastened along to the river in which I saw a struggling mass of men and horses from whom little streams of blood was coloring the water near them. Lieutenant Hodgson was one of the number and had just been wounded, so I heard him say. I turned my horse a little to the right to avoid the crowd and, jumping him into the river, was soon across.

After a hard struggle I climbed the steep bank, the rapid pace and exertion over the river had completely exhausted my horse and he stood trembling with fatigue and refused to go any further. He was a poor, broken-winded beast at the best, and was to have been condemned long ago but a shortage of mounts made it necessary to take him along. As I was a late comer in that Troop, he was assigned to me, and bore the name of Steamboat, because of the particular noise he made when traveling.

I dismounted and amid whistling of bullets stood there for a few

The revolver that dropped to the ground while Taylor was trying to steady himself and his horse was identical to this Colt Model U.S. 1873, a single-action .45-caliber Army revolver.

the bluff where I found the greater part of Reno's command, we were soon joined by a few others who barely succeeded in making their escape.

In times past I had wondered how a man felt, when he believed that almost inevitable, sudden death was upon him, I knew it now, for our escape was little less than miraculous when one considers the overwhelming number of Indians and the pitifully disorganized condition in which we made our death encircled ride in the valley and up the bluffs, pursued by a howling mass of red warriors, naked to the waist, who maddened and desperate by the terrified cries of their wives and children whose lives were put in jeopardy for the third time within a few weeks rushed from their camps and careing nothing for their own lives were determined to save their families, or die.

They seemed to us, in all their hideousness of paint and feathers, and wild fierce cries, like fiends incarnate, but were they?

moments waiting for him to get his breath. Then I tried to lead him along but he would not budge a foot. Getting in his rear, I jabbed him with my gun in vain while my comrades were rushing by the bluffs, some mounted, others on foot leading their horses, disappearing over the top. Things looked serious indeed, for to be dismounted in the face of hundreds of Sioux warriors but a short distance away, was like looking into your grave.

In my anger and disgust I gave the beast a parting kick, unslung my carbine and started up the bluff, a mark as I thought for hundreds of rifles, little puffs of dust rising from the ground all around as the bullets buried themselves in the dry dusty hillside. The slope which we were ascending was a funnel shaped ridge, the small end being near the top of the bluff, with narrow, deep ravines on either side terminating within a few yards of the river. It must have been providence that directed us to that particular spot for there was no other place anywhere near that we could have made the ascent with so much haste and so little trouble.

I had gone perhaps one third of the way up when I was overtaken by a dismounted comrade of my old Troop, [M] named Myers, "Tinker Bill" we used to call him from the fact of his having been a tinner's apprentice before his enlistment. We walked along quite close together for a few feet when with but the single exclamation of "Oh," Myers pitched forward face down to the ground. I bent over him but he was dead, shot between the left ear and eye. It may be my turn next I thought and instead of keeping straight ahead I bore off to the right a little and more into the ravine. Then turned again to the left, zig-zagging as it were but ever going up. When, within a short distance of the top, I was overtaken by a former comrade of M Troop, Frank Neeley. He was mounted and had a led horse with him. This horse he turned over to me, very glad to get rid of his charge. It was with a deep feeling of relief that I got into a saddle again for my chances were a little better now, although my new mount was not such a very great improvement over the one I had left behind. This one was called "Old Dutch," and he was all that the name would imply; still I was not "looking in his mouth", he was a horse. So I mounted and rode on over the top of the bluff where I found the greater part of Reno's command. We were soon joined by a few others who barely suc-ceeded in making their escape.

In times past I have wondered how a man felt, when he believed that almost inevitable, sudden death was upon him. I knew it now, for our escape was little less than miraculous when one considers the overwhelming number of Indians and the pitifully disorganized condition in which we made our death-encircled ride in the valley and up the bluffs, pursued by a howling mass of red warriors, naked to the waist, who, maddened and desperate by the terrified cries of their wives and children whose lives were put in jeopardy for the third time within a few weeks, rushed from their camps and, caring nothing for their own lives, were determined to save their families, or die.

They seemed to us, in all their hideousness of paint and feathers, and wild fierce cries, like fiends incarnate, but were they?

CHAPTER V

Besieged on the Bluff

The fire and pursuit by the Indians seemed to cease as soon as we reached the top of the bluffs, this was much to be thankful for although we little dreamed of the cause.

Major Reno was walking around in an excited manner. He had lost his hat during the "charge" and had bound a red handkerchief about his head, which gave him a rather peculiar and unmilitary appearance. Most of the men had thrown themselves on the ground to rest for they were well nigh exhausted. The officers were talking together, comparing notes and so forth. We had been there but a very short time when we were joined by Captain Benteen with the three Troops, H, D, and K, that had been sent off to the left some two hours before. They were now, in obedience to a written as well as verbal order, on their way to join Custer.

This junction with all of Reno's command occurred at "2:30 p.m.," so Reno states. A very short time afterwards, Captain McDougall with B Troop, escorting the pack train, came along and joined us. Captain McDougall had also received an order from General Custer to make haste and join him with the pack train. The message to McDougall was delivered to him by Sergeant David C. Kanipe of Captain Tom Custer's Troop, C. It might be well to say here that Boston Custer, a younger brother of the General, was acting as a civilian forage master. He had been riding with the Gen-

"In the darkness a deep feeling of sadness came over our hearts. Scattered around us near by were the fresh, and shallow graves of some who had fallen in our midst that afternoon and had just been covered by their comrades."

eral that morning but had gone back to the pack train for a fresh horse, which having secured he started on ahead to rejoin the General's command. While on his way he met Trumpeter Martin[i] who was bringing a dispatch to Captain Benteen. Mr. Custer and the Trumpeter exchanged a few words and then continued their respective ways. Mr. Custer had time enough to rejoin the command before the battle began and his body was found within a few yards of those of his two brothers.

For over two hours after the arrival of Captain Benteen's command we remained there on the bluff, unmolested in any manner. The First-Sergeants of Reno's three Troops went around checking on the men present so as to know how many had been killed, wounded, or missing, and also taking an account of government property lost. We had heard firing off in the general direction Custer was supposed to have gone. "Why don't we move?", was a question asked by more than one. The three Troops that had been engaged in the valley were it is true somewhat demoralized, but that was no excuse for the whole command to remain inactive. A few of our men had been wounded, but none so seriously that they could not ride with the pack train. All of the officers must have known that Custer was engaged with the Indians and quite near by for he had not time to go a great way. The sudden withdrawal of that strong force of Indians who had driven us from the close vicinity of their camp, could indicate but one thing, and that was another attack on their camp, real or theatened, by a force from another direction.[1]

In the latter part of the afternoon, not far from half-past four, a squad of twelve of our comrades were seen coming up the bluffs. Some of them had become dismounted in the woods or just outside when the command left and they remained hidden in the woods, strange as it may seem, until all the Indians appeared to have left that vicinity, when they came out and on foot started in the direction Reno had been seen to take. There was fourteen of the party altogether while in the woods but two of them refused to take the chances of escaping in the daylight and remained behind. They were afterwards discovered by the Indians and killed.

The party that escaped consisted of George Herendeen,[2] a scout, six

1. Ed. note: Benteen believed that Custer's troops had been annihilated before his battalion joined Reno's command on the bluffs. See *Reno Court of Inquiry*, p. 334.
2. See Appendix I for Herendeen's account.

soldiers of G Troop, three of M and two of A. While on their way they saw but five Indians whom they drove off with little trouble and no loss. After they had crossed the river, which was waist deep, one of the A Troop men found and recognized my horse grazing unconcernedly where I had left him. He brought the horse along, later on turning him over to me, who, he had supposed, was killed. Not an article of my equipment or belongings was missing although the horse had been for nearly three hours quite near, if not within the Indian line.

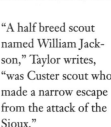

I may state right here that another party of our men had also remained in the woods. Unseen and unknown by the party just mentioned, this second party consisted of Lieutenant De Rudio, Private Tom O'Neil of G Troop, Frank Girard, the Interpreter for the "Ree" scouts, and a half-breed scout named William Jackson. These four, after many narrow escapes and an absence of about thirty four hours, reached our lines late in the evening of the 26th, making altogether eighteen men known to have been left behind when the charge was made. It is quite likely that there were several others who failed to escape.

"A half breed scout named William Jackson," Taylor writes, "was Custer scout who made a narrow escape from the attack of the Sioux."

Soon after the party of twelve rejoined us and somewhere near five o'clock we had orders to "fall in", and mounting our horses we started in the direction Custer was believed to have gone. A very short ride along the side of the bluffs that shut off our view of the Indian village brought us to a ridge that afforded a partial view of what was afterwards found to be Custer's battlefield. Many Indians were seen in the distance, and others nearer by. Soon they began to come in our direction and our advance Troop under Captain Weir was attacked.[3]

The whole command was then ordered to retire and we returned to the place we had left a short time before. By this time the Indians had us completely surrounded and opened a furious fire. The pack train, wounded,

3. Ed. note: Captain Weir made an abortive attempt to lead a portion of Reno's command in the direction Custer had taken but was quickly repulsed by Indians returning from the Custer battlefield.

and horses were placed in a depression between two ridges on top of which the men were posted, lying close to the ground. This was, according to my belief, about six o'clock, and that is the time set by Major Reno in his report. Captain Godfrey seems to think it was a little later but he must be mistaken for it certainly never took us two hours to travel about one mile and return to our starting place, especially when urged on by the advancing Sioux for whose power we were entertaining a greater respect than had formerly prevailed.

Two good sized ridges sloping from the steep bluffs that overhung the river back toward the east formed the depression that afforded some shelter for our horses and wounded, although it was subjected to a constant long range fire from the east. Those whose lot it was to hold the horses lay just as close to the ground as they could, wishing most fervently for night to come for the day had been a very strenuous one and full to the utmost with danger that blanched the cheeks of officers and men, the veterans of many battles as well as the raw recruit that was but a few weeks in the Regiment. In later years when thinking of our position on the hill and the generally demoralized condition of the command, it has been to me a great wonder why that strong force of Indians that had swept over and annihilated Custer with his five Troops in such a brief time should have hesitated to pursue the tactics that won for them such a great victory an hour or two before. It was indeed most fortunate for us that they did not.

The firing, however, was continuous on the part of the Indians until dusk and after that a few scattering shots, ceasing altogether about nine o'clock. Our casualties since taking position on the hill has been, Captain Godfrey says, "comparatively few." Personally, I knew of but three killed, and a few more, wounded.

After it got dark some scouts were sent out to look for signs of Custer's command. They returned in a very short time and in considerable haste saying "the country was full of Indians." A Trumpeter was ordered to a little eminence to sound some calls which it was hoped might reach the ears of Custer's command and so direct them to our position. Facing the direction in which Custer had gone, three or four calls were blown with all the force the Trumpeter could give, the last, as I remember it, was "Taps", a call blown after "Tattoo", to put out the lights, and also always sounded over the grave of a soldier at the time of his burial.

Was it not something more than mere chance which led the Trumpeter to send out on the still night air the notes of "Lights all out"? And as the echoes floated away in the darkness a deep feeling of sadness came over our hearts. Scattered around us near by were the fresh, and shallow graves of some who had fallen in our midst that afternoon and had just been covered by their comrades. No ceremony, a little trench right where they fell, a few inches of earth thrown over them, to be washed off by the first rain.

Down in the valley, near the woods, and along the steep hillside lay others of our command unburied, men who fell in that headlong retreat. Still farther away but unknown to us then, were the mangled remains of over two hundred of our Regiment. It now seems most fitting that "Taps" should have been blown at that time, unthinkingly, but how appropriately, no answering call came to our anxious ears. The personal loss of intimate comrades, the great disaster to our Regiment, and our own narrow escape had a very sobering effect on all.

*   *   *

And now comes a rather peculiar incident, one that some may be tempted to question but which I aver to be strictly true. After the fire of the Indians had ceased altogether the men, glad to be relieved of the terrible strain of the last few hours, moved about quite freely and were naturally anxious to know what our next move would be. The First-Sergeant of company A having been wounded, his duties fell upon Sergeant Feihler, an elderly German of a rather placid nature. Our Company was considerably scattered and then I saw Sergeant Feihler near the low end of the herded horses and pack mules. I approached and said to him. "What are we going to do, stay here all night, or try to move away?" Major Reno was then standing quite near, and heard my question. He turned at once, with the remark, "I would like to know how in

Hell we are going to move away?" I was quite surprised at his words and manner, but as I had certain ideas in my mind, I continued to Sergeant Feihler that "if we are going to stay here we ought to be making some kind of a barricade, for the Indians would be at us the first thing in the morning." Major Reno, who was still there, spoke up at once, saying, "Yes, Sergeant, that is a good idea. Set all the men you can to work, right away." Sergeant Feihler then began to order men to take boxes of hardtack, packsaddles, sides of bacon, dead mules and horses, in fact anything they could use, and make a barricade across the lower part of the depression. This was finally done, but not without a great deal of entreaty and urging by the Sergeant. For strange as it may seem, very many of the men showed but little interest in the work, and the officers, less. The only excuse I can offer for this seeming indifference was that they doubtless expected that General Custer would make his appearance during the night and that our labor would be wasted. That barricade proved of the greatest service to us the next day, saving the lives undoubtedly of many of the men who were not slow to seek its protection from the merciless fire opened on us the next morning. Commanding, as it did, the only feasible approach for a mounted charge against our lines, one of which the Indians started to make the next day, they met with such a warm reception at the very beginning that they gave up the idea at this point. Had it not been for this barricade it is my firm belief that they would have rode over us as they did over Custer's men.

I do not know if Companies, M, K, B, and D, made any special attempts at this time, to fortify their position, but I saw no evidence of its being done, and as for "H," Troop, I know that they did not.

Soon after our barricade was completed and not far from ten O'clock, p.m. I was detailed as picket guard. There were six Privates and one Corporal, the latter was Stanislaus Roy, all out of A Troop. We were advanced about three hundred yards down the slope in front of our breastworks, where two sentinels were quickly posted, one on the right and the other about one hundred yards to the left. A short distance in front of us were two hillocks some fifty yards apart, behind which of course we could not see.

But they were used that afternoon and the next day as an advantageous place to pick off any of our men who recklessly exposed themselves.

I was assigned as the second relief and so had a chance to sleep for two hours before my turn came. But before lying down I scrutinized as carefully as I could all the features of the landscape in front, especially the taller growth of sagebrush that might be mistaken in the dark for the stealthy approach of an Indian. Satisfied that I had the bearings pretty well in mind I lay down and in a moment was fast asleep, a deep, untroubled sleep, of which we were all greatly in need, having had but little the night before. It seemed like a very short two hours when I was awakened and went out to relieve the first sentinel who duly reported, "All's well". I took a position a little different from the one the other sentinel had, and sat down to watch, for walking would have made one rather conspicuous. The shouting and sound of the drums in the camps of the Indians could still be heard.

It had been a day of intense excitement, of desperate struggle and final triumph, such a day they had never known before. The sudden appearance of the soldiers at the very edge of their camp, the rally of the warriors in defense of their homes, the defeat of the white men, of whom over two hundred lay cold in death on the plains and hills near by, a tribute to the prowess of the Indian. And what a booty had fallen into their hands, everything that a horseman needed. Horses, saddles, blankets, and the arms, over 200 carbines, as many revolvers, and ammunition to fit, money, and all kinds of clothing. There was indeed much cause for rejoicing and the "dancing of Scalps." But it was not all exultation. In many a lodge lay a cold red form brought from the near by field of battle, the lifeless form of a husband and father who had rode out so bravely but a few hours before to defend all that he had in life, his wife and children, and a little skin covered lodge. In other tepees, stretched out on a pile of robes lay some helpless from serious wounds, some even fast approaching the ghost land of their fathers, and bearing with the stolid indifference of the race their coming fate. For those who were dead there was loud lamentations, wailing deep and sincere, such was their custom.

At one time during the night amidst the savage yells and discordant noise of the Indian drums we heard the sound of a bugle and it brought us all to our feet at once. "Custer was coming at last," was our first thought. We listened, again the notes of a bugle was borne to our eager ears, this time a little more distinct. But it was not an army call that I had ever heard or was familiar with at least. Though some declared it was. One thing was quite evident, it came from the camp of our foes below us. From where, as if to mock our budding hopes, came a renewed vigor to the beating of the drums and another and louder outburst of the wolf-like yells.

The explanation was not hard for us then, for we remembered that one of the Trumpeters of G Troop had been killed in the bottom on our retreat and the Indians had undoubtedly possessed themselves of his bugle and were amusing their fellows and adding to the general din. That there was then probably eight or ten more bugles in the Indian camp, taken from Custer's five Troops, (each troop being allowed two), was something that could not have entered our minds.

Many speculations have since been indulged in regarding this bugle episode. One theory being that some half-breed or Indian, who in the past had frequented some army post and become rather friendly with Trumpeter, had learned to blow a few calls, or something like them. Another theory was that one of Custer's Trumpeters had been taken prisoner and before being put to death was allowed, or else compelled to blow the bugle. To my mind, the most reasonable explanation is the one first given.

My two hours duty passed quickly, the shouting and sound of the drums in the Indian camps were growing fainter and nothing more was heard except the long drawn-out and mournful howl of a prairie wolf over in the direction Custer had taken. When the third relief came on I reported, "All's well," and again sought the soldier's couch, the rough hard ground, and as before was soon fast asleep.

My next awakening was in the early dawn as I had expected it would be. For about three o'clock just as it was growing light there came two rifle shots from a low ridge in our front. This may have been the Indians' signal to open fire, for in less time than it takes to write about it a perfect shower of bullets followed from all along their line. It was hardly necessary for the Corporal to order us back to our lines. We went and went quickly, and on our arrival threw ourselves down behind the breastworks, the construction of which was now showing its wisdom. Besides the greater part of A Troop engaged in holding this line of defense the force consisted of a number of stragglers from other Troops and several citizen packers. At one time during the day, I observed an officer whose company was in another part of the field, and one more perilous than ours, safely sheltering himself behind the thickest part of our breastworks.

CHAPTER VI

Terry Raises the Siege

"In many a lodge lay a cold red form brought from the near by field of battle, the lifeless form of a husband and father who had rode out so bravely but a few hours before to defend all that he had in life, his wife and children, and a little skin covered lodge."

From the time the Indians began firing early in the morning until late in the forenoon, there was no time that it was prudent for a man to raise his head above the barricade. Not that the Indians kept up a continuous fire, their ammunition was too costly for that. But let a man stand up, or expose even a small part of his body and the act was followed by a shower of bullets which, however, did not always hit their mark as the following incident will show.

Captain Benteen, who has been criticized for not being more prompt in obeying Custer's orders,[1] was nevertheless one of the bravest acting men of our entire command. His Troop was holding a position on a ridge to the right of our breastworks, and a few hundred yards south, as near as I can recall the points of compass. They had neglected to dig any pits or make any other provision for shelter from the fire, which an old soldier like Captain Benteen must have known would be directed against his line the next morning. Therefore, owing to their exposed position, they suffered quite severely in [number] of wounded, no less than ten, and one account says eighteen men were wounded, and three killed outright. As a result, Captain Benteen came over to where our line was and asked Captain Moylan for some of the material our barricade was made of, the barricade being a little longer than was necessary for the number of men behind it.

All this time Captain Benteen was in full view of the Indians, making

---

1. Ed. note: For a recent study of Benteen's movements that seems to add credence to this criticism, see John S. Gray, *Custer's Last Campaign*, pp. 258–64.

no effort whatever to seek any shelter. You could see the bullets throwing up dust as they struck all around him while he, as calmly as if on parade, came down to our lines and, after his errand, returned in the same manner carrying in his hand a carbine, with which I observed him measuring the distance from his foot to a point where a bullet had just entered the ground in his front less than two feet away.

This incident was impressed on my mind by the fact that I was in the same zone of fire, being but a short distance from him at the time. I was one of the party detailed to carry up some material for Benteen's breastworks, and with a box of hardtack on my shoulder was hurrying up the ridge. It was a trying time and when a bullet crashed into the box on my shoulder, nearly knocking it off, I had some doubts about ever finishing the trip, short as it was. But I did and unharmed.

When we started back to our own Company we took a circle around more to our rear and in a little less exposed position. I had but just reached my place behind the works when the man next to me on the left, and whom I could almost touch without moving, raised his head just enough to take a shot when a bullet struck him right between the eyes. It was instant and pain-less death for he did not make a move or a sound. This man was one of the citizen packers named Frank Mann. He had been quite noticeable for his continuous firing without any apparent cause or result, and had been warned not to expose himself so much. But the warning was of no effect and he was finally located by an Indian sharpshooter and put out of business.

A few moments afterwards another comrade and myself moved the body back a few feet, for it was too suggestive lying there between us, and as I had lost my own revolver I took the one carried by the packer, it being of Government issue and of no more use to him while it might be of great ser-vice to me at any moment. Life seemed very attractive throughout that eventful day for such close acquaintance with death is not a pleasing sensa-tion, and I think that most of the soldiers felt that unless a special providence interfered we were certainly doomed.

* * *

During the forenoon Captain Benteen went over to the north side where Major Reno was and asked him for reinforcements. He believed that the Indians would soon charge his position, and as he has but one troop [H] to hold the south line, the chances were that if the Indians did make a rush they would run right over the few men left in his Company and have all the rest of us between two fires. After some urging Reno finally ordered Captain French to take his troop [M] over to the south side.

Soon after the arrival of M Troop, Benteen ordered a charge and succeeded in driving the Indians from his front nearly to the river. A number of the soldiers were wounded but only one seriously. And that was Private Tanner of M Troop who fell a short way down the hill. After the charge, a party of his comrades rushed down the slope, rolled him on a blanket and amidst a severe fire bore him back to the lines where he died soon afterwards.

The firing would almost cease at times and then begin again more furious than ever, but it finally slackened toward noon and a call was made for volunteers to go to the river after water which we had been without for many hours. There is no questioning the fact that the thirst of many was intense, but I do doubt that there was any real suffering unless it was in the case of some of the wounded. Still it was not pleasant to go twenty-four hours without a drink of water, especially on a hot day in June while within a few hundred yards flowed a river of clear cool water, and off to the southwest could be seen the snow topped range of the Bighorn mountains, seemingly but a short distance.

Various expedients had been tried to alleviate our thirst; chewing lead from a bullet and the inner part of the thick leaves of the prickly pear, holding pebbles in the mouth, etc. All were useless, if not an aggravation. The call for volunteers met with a quick and full response; and covered by some of the best marksmen in the front of Benteen's line, a party with camp kettles and canteens made their way down a ravine that approached within a few yards of the river. Then, making a rush, they reached the river, filled the kettles and hastened back to the ravine where the canteens were filled.

Some Indians stationed near by on the opposite side opened fire as soon as a man appeared, making the undertaking a very hazardous one and several of the men were wounded, one of them so badly that one of his legs had to be amputated. This man was Michael Madden, a Saddler of K Troop. This undertaking seemed to me at the time a foolish one and uncalled for under the circumstances. The almost dead certainty of putting five or six men *hors de combat* at a time when every man was needed who could fire a gun, was not, in my opinion, justified in any way by the exigencies of the case.

In the course of an hour or two afterwards most of the Indians appeared to have left. But I think this was their last card and they were in hopes of throwing us off our guard, for about two o'clock they reopened fire and drove us all to our shelter. This last attack was not of long duration, for after a time the firing ceased altogether. They later set fire to the grass in the bottom and shortly afterwards a great mass of Indians were seen in motion going up the valley in the direction of the Bighorn Mountains. It was a most joyful sight to us for we had spent the better part of two days in a decidedly nerve-strained condition and I doubt if a dirtier, more haggard looking lot of men ever wore the Army blue than that little remnant of the once proud Seventh.

It was fast approaching twilight when Major Reno decided to change his position to one nearer the river. The men were set to work digging pits with the expectation of still more fighting; and, besides, the stench from the dead men and horses was becoming very offensive. It did not now take so much urging, they had learned a lesson and in a few hours we had some pretty fair pits constructed, which, I have been informed, are still to be seen.[2] The one upon which I worked was circular in form and room enough in it for six or eight men. Our tools were tin cups and plates, knives, sharpened paddles made out of pieces of hardtack boxes, and a few shovels.

With relaxed nerves and tired bodies we stretched ourselves out on the bare ground for the first good, whole night's rest since the 23rd. Sometime during the night four of our missing comrades showed up in two separate parties. Lieutenant DeRudio and Private Tom O'Neil of G Troop came in about twelve o'clock, while Frank Girard, the interpreter, and a half-breed

2. Ed. note: They are still visible today.

scout named [William "Billy"] Jackson came along at some other hour. They had been left in the bottom like many others when Reno made his retreat and were quite fortunate in finding us, and very happy also. They had been concealed in the woods along the river since two o'clock p.m. of the 25th in close proximity to the Indians who were on their way to and from our beleaguered lines.

*　*　*

Tuesday morning June 27th, found us up bright and early eating in peace our breakfast of bacon, hardtack and coffee. We watered our horses who acted as if they would never get enough, washed our faces and hands and straightened ourselves up generally. Not an Indian was in sight and no shots were fired to keep us ducking. Major Reno seemed determined to stay where he was and kept the men in readiness to occupy the pits should the Indians return.

About the middle of the forenoon a cloud of dust appeared down the river and we half expected a renewal of the fight. The horses were secured, water brought up and we awaited the coming of whatever it might be. Soon a scout appeared with a note from General Terry to General Custer. The scout was soon followed by Lieutenant Bradley of the Montana Column and his detachment of scouts from whose lips came the first news of the terrible disaster that had befallen Custer's command, which we were even then hoping might be the cause of the dust cloud coming up the valley. This however, proved to be the Montana Column, accompanied by General Terry, who with General Gibbon and several other officers were shortly in our midst. Captain Godfrey says, "their coming was greeted with prolonged cheers, the grave countenance of the General awed the men to silence, the officers assembled to meet their guests, there was scarcely a dry eye, hardly a word was spoken, but quivering lips and hearty grasping of hand gave token of thankfulness for the relief, and grief for the misfortune."

General Gibbon's command soon arrived at a point in the valley nearly opposite our position and went into camp. One of his officers, Lieutenant Coolidge of the Seventh Infantry, who had some medical experience, was sent up to assist Dr. Porter in the care of our wounded of whom there were some fifty-two. The wounded were moved as soon as possible to the camp of the Montana Column. This work was rather difficult in the case of those who were seriously injured and helpless, for they had to be carried in blankets down a steep bluff and then through a river that was nearly waist deep. The men exercised all the care and consideration that they could, but it must have been a great relief to the wounded when safely deposited in their new "field hospital," a grassy bed, protected from the sun by a piece of shelter-tent.

The rest of the day was spent in collecting our effects, destroying all surplus property that could not be taken along and which might be of some use to the Indians, gathering up the bacon and hardtack, and other useful material from the barricade, besides dispatching a number of badly wounded horses and mules. During the day I went over in front of Benteen's position, where, down the slope a few yards, lay the body of that recklessly brave warrior who had tried to count a coup[3] on one of Benteen's men. I had seen quite a number of the "quick" ones, and at last was to gaze on a "dead" one. There were but two left on our field, one near the ford where we ascended the bluff, and this one.

In a little depression there lay outstretched a stalwart Sioux warrior, stark naked with the exception of a breech clout and moccasins. He lay with his head up the hill, his right arm extended in the direction the fatal shot had come, a look of grim defiance on his face, which was not disfigured with the streaks of yellow, green, and crimson, so common to many. Perhaps in his hurry to get into the fight he could not stop to don his war paint. He had been scalped by some soldier,[4] the greatest misfortune that could happen, for thereby his soul was annihilated; such was the belief of his people, and for him now there was no Happy Hunting Ground. Never had I seen a more perfect specimen of physical manhood, he must have been about thirty years old, nearly if not quite six feet in height and of splendid proportions. He looked like a bronze statue that had been thrown to the ground. It was such a form that MacMonnies[5] might have had for a model when he sculptured

3. Ed. note: To "count coup" meant to touch an enemy's body in battle. This was considered a greater feat of bravery than simply killing him, which could be accomplished from a distance.
4. Ed. note: This practice was fairly common among soldiers who had spent some time in the West, but quite the opposite with raw recruits.
5. Ed. note: Frederick William MacMonnies (1833–1937).

WITH CUSTER ON THE LITTLE BIGHORN

"The Last Arrow". I could not help a feeling of sorrow as I stood gazing upon him. He was within a few hundred rods of his home and family which we had attempted to destroy and he had died to defend. The home of his slayer was perhaps a thousand miles away. In a few days the wolves and buzzards would have his remains torn asunder and scattered, for the soldiers had no disposition to bury a dead Indian, and his family and tribe were even then in full retreat.

I have since learned that his name was High Elk. His medicine bag, which was all the property he had left on him I brought away as a souvenir of a very brave man in a memorable battle. It was carried on a belt and was made from the leather of a bootleg, fashioned in shape and size like a pistol cartridge box, and sewed together with fine wire, the flap studded with brass tacks. Among its contents were three little parcels of different colored dry paint, each done up in a piece of soft buckskin, a piece of dry flagroot, part of a coarse comb, a few matches and some thread and needles. I have often wondered since that day, if, in a few years after his bleached and scattered bones were not found by the Superintendent of the Custer National Cemetery who might quite naturally think that they were the remains of some of Reno's command that had been overlooked by the first burial party. And so he might have had them gathered up and buried among those whom he had fought against.

The remark, credited to an Army officer that "the only good Indian, was a dead Indian",[6] may have inspired the following lines by Hartley Alexander:

6. Ed. note: This quote has been attributed to both General Philip Sheridan and General William T. Sherman. Regardless of who said it, the quote reflects the government attitude toward the Indians during this era.

The Only Good Indian

So there he lies, redeemed at last!
His knees drawn tense, just as he fell
and shrieked out his soul in a battle-yell;
One hand with the rifle still clutched fast;
One stretched straight out, the fingers clenched
In the knotted roots of the sun bleached grass;
His head flung back on the tangled mass
Of raven mane, with the war-plume wretched
Awry and torn; the painted face
Still forwards turned, the white teeth bare
Twixt the livid lips, the wide eyed glare,
The bronze cheek gaped by battle-trace
In dying rage rent fresh apart—
A strange expression for one all good:
On his naked breast a splotch of blood
Where the lead evangel cleft his heart.
So there he lies, at last made whole,
Regenerate! Christ rest his soul!

[CHAPTER VII]

Custer's Advance

We will now return to General Custer, whose subsequent movements after leaving Reno are but little known. After crossing the divide between the Rosebud and the Little Bighorn, and somewhere about noon, the Regiment had been divided into Battalions. Custer retaining under his personal command, five Troops: Troop C under Captain T. W. Custer, and Lieutenant Harrington; Troop E [Gray Horse], Lieutenants Smith and Sturgis; Troop F Captain Yates and Lieutenant Van Reily; Troop I. Captain Keogh and Lieutenant Porter; Troop L Lieutenants Calhoun and Crittenden. Lieutenant W.W. Cook was Adjutant, and Dr. G. E. Lord was the medical officer [Regimental Surgeon]. There was an average of 37 enlisted men to a troop.[1] Thirteen commissioned officers, counting Dr. Lord, three civilians; Boston Custer, a brother of the General, Autie Reed a nephew, and Mark Kellogg, a reporter; four non commissioned officers on the General's staff; one interpreter, Mitch Bouyer; a half-breed and one Crow scout, Curley, making a total force of 206 men, not counting the Crow scout. Captain Godfrey in describing the burial of Custer's command says that according to his memoranda, "we buried 212 bodies". If he is correct there were probably some six or eight more enlisted men than have been given above.

The two commands, Custer's and Reno's, continued until about 12:30 p.m. when they were within about two miles of the river. Reno was then ordered to "Move forward at as rapid a gait as prudent and charge afterwards." Custer soon left the trail and moved squarely to the right, apparently

1. According to a list of casualties published in the New York *Herald*.

Curley, a Crow scout, came under General Custer's personal command. This photo was taken from an old postcard.

2. Ed. note: Much has been written regarding this event suggesting that rather than cheering Reno's battalion on, Custer was attempting to signal Reno to abort the charge, for he had seen from the bluffs what a large number of Indians Reno was up against.
3. Inexplicably, the author switched, temporarily, to the present tense.

heading for the lower part of the Indian village. His next, and final appearance was on a high point of the bluffs overlooking the river and the Indian camps, a short distance below the point where Reno's command made their hurried and difficult ascent. This occurred while Reno's Battalion was charging down the valley and, just before he dismounted, the command to fight on foot. Custer was seen to wave his hat to the charging Battalion, a signal of encouragement, and a final farewell. What a picture it must have been, and what a pity some artist could not reproduce it on canvas.[2]

Custer and his staff on a point of the high, precipitous bluffs were gazing intently at the scene in the valley, at their feet almost, the tortuous and heavily timbered river across which and directly in front of them, was the outskirts of the Indian village. The valley, a good half mile wide and stretching away for miles was filled with innumerable tepees of the Indians—the hosts of excited warriors rushing from all directions to meet the unexpected foe, the pony herds being driven in, and the squaws and children hurrying down the valley in great disorder and dodging the oncoming warriors.

Charging down the valley from the south, and close by, in a line of battle that stretches nearly across the bottom, come a Battalion of Cavalry [three troops] flanked on the left by a number of friendly Indian scouts. On the slope of the bluffs to the right and rear of Custer, perhaps two hundred yards away, and moving in a column of four rapidly to the northward is Custer's own Battalion of cavalry, five troops.[3]

* * *

At this point, Custer dispatched two messengers. One, Daniel A. Kanipe, a Sergeant of C Troop, was sent back to Captain McDougall who, with his troop B was escorting the pack train. His message was to "go to Captain

McDougall, tell him to bring the pack train straight across the country, if any packs come loose, cut them; and come on quick; a big Indian camp. If you see Captain Benteen tell him to come quick, a big Indian camp."

About the same time Trumpeter John Martini, of H Troop, who was Custer's Orderly Bugler, was given a written message to carry to Captain Benteen, which read:

> "Benteen,
> Come on, Big Village,
> Be quick, bring packs.
> W.W. Cooke
> P.S. bring packs."

These were the last messages, orders, or knowledge that our command had of the living Custer.

*   *   *

As Captain Benteen has been quite generally criticized for his failure to obey General Custer's last order, it seems like a fitting place to give Benteen's report of the movements of his Battalion as copied from the Report of Secretary of War for the year 1876. This Report was made to Major Reno while in camp on the Yellowstone.

3Bb.-Report of Capt. F.W. Benteen.
Camp Seventh Cavalry, July 4 1876.

Sir. In obedience to verbal instructions received from you, I have the honor to report the operations of my battalion, consisting of Companies D, H, and K, on the 25th ultimo.

The directions I received from Lt-Colonel Custer were, to move with my command to the left, to send a well-mounted officer with about six men who should ride rapidly to a line of bluffs about five miles to our left and front, with instructions to report at once to me if anything of Indians could be seen from that point. I was to follow the movement of this detachment as rapidly as possible. Lieutenant Gibson was the officer selected, and I followed closely with the battalion, at times getting in advance of the detachment. The bluffs designated were gained, but nothing seen but other bluffs quite as large and precipitous as were before me. I kept on to those and the country was the same, there being no valley of any kind that I could see on any side. I had then gone about fully ten miles; the ground was terribly hard on horses, so I determined to carry out the other instructions, which were, that if in my judgement there was nothing to be seen of Indians, valley, etc., in the direction I was going, to return with the battalion to the trail the command was following. I accordingly did so, reaching the trail just in advance of the pack train. I pushed rapidly on, soon getting out of sight of the advance of the train, until reaching a morass, I halted to water the animals, who had been without water since about 8 p.m. of the day before. This watering did not occasion the loss of 15 minutes, and when I was moving out the advance of the train commenced watering from that morass. I went at a slow trot until I came to a burning lodge with the dead body of an Indian in it on a scaffold. We did not halt. About a mile farther on I met a sergeant of the regiment with orders from Lieutenant Colonel Custer to the officer in charge of the rear guard and train to bring it to the front with as great rapidity as was possible. Another mile on I met Trumpeter Morton [Martini], of my own company, with a written order from First-Lieut. W.W. Cook[e] to me, which read;

"Benteen, Come on, Big village, Be quick, bring packs.
W.W. Cooke   P.S. bring packs."

I could then see no movement of any kind in any direction; a horse on the hill, riderless, being the only living thing I could see in my front. I inquired of the trumpeter, what had been done, and he informed [me] that the Indians had "skedaddled", abandoning the village. Another mile and a half brought me in sight of the stream and plain in which were some of our dismounted men fighting, and the Indians charging and recharging them in great numbers. The plain seemed to be alive with them. I then noticed our men in large numbers running for the bluffs on the right bank of the stream. I concluded at once that those had been repulsed, and was of the opinion that if I crossed the ford with my battalion, that I should have it treated in like manner; for, from long experience with cavalry, I judge there were 900 veteran Indians right there at that time, against which the large element of recruits in my battalion would stand no earthly chance as mounted men. I then moved up to the bluffs and reported my command to Maj. M.A. Reno. I did not return for the pack train because I deemed it perfectly safe where it was, and we could defend it, had it been threatened, from our position on the bluff; and another thing, it savored too much of coffee-cooling to return when I was sure a fight was progressing in the front, and deeming the train as safe without me.

Very Respectfully,   F. W. Benteen
                                Captain Seventh Cavalry.
Lieut-Geo. D. Wallace
Adjutant Seventh Cavalry.[4]

Captain Benteen's presence so close to the river while presumably under the guidance of Trumpeter Martini who had left Custer but a short time before, is to my mind the strongest evidence of Custer's probable route. Captain Godfrey who was in command of K Troop and with Benteen's battalion, says, "during our march on the left we could see occasionally the battalion under Custer, distinguished by the troop mounted on gray horses, [E] two or three times we heard loud cheering, and also some fews shots." [Reno's Command] Not knowing anything as to the exact whereabouts of the other battalions when he arrived in sight of the river and saw that an engagement was in progress, Benteen might very naturally think it was Custer's command until he came into close touch with the retreating soldiers on the bluffs; and then whatever his inclinations may have been in regard to obeying Custer's orders, he was, after coming in contact with Major Reno, subordinate to that officer,

4. Ed. note: Report made July 4, 1876, to Major Reno. In Executive Document 1, Part 2, House of Representatives, 44th Congress, 2nd Session.

and therefore obliged to obey the Major's orders, which, under the circumstances, it can easily be surmised were to remain where he was for the present.

Custer, after seeing what he did from his position on the bluffs, must have realized at once that there was but one course to pursue, and that was to get into the fight at some effective point and as soon as possible. At his present position a line of steep high bluffs separated him from the river on the other side of which lay the Indian camps. A short distance on his right front was a dry creek which ran into the river opposite the Indian camps, and it must have suggested, as it afterwards proved, a fording place.[5] Still farther away to the right, running parallel with the river and not quite a mile from it was a ridge, much lower than the bluffs but still the highest point in the immediate vicinity. There is a difference of opinion as to what course Custer took from the point where he saw the village and dispatched his messengers. Some claim that he followed the ridge spoken of until nearly opposite the lower or northern end of the village, when he was furiously attacked by the warriors who came out to meet him. Others hold that he followed the dry creek down trying to find a crossing place and when near the river was met with such an overwhelming fire that he had to fall back to the ridge which seemed to offer the best chance for a successful defence.

If this last theory is correct, it is the one I have been inclined to believe in, for two reasons. First, General Terry's Report,[6] which says of Custer, . . . "his trail, from the point where Reno crossed the stream, passes along and in rear of the crests of the bluffs on the right bank for nearly of quite three miles, then it comes down to the bank of the river, but at once diverges from it as if he had unsuccessfully attempted to cross, then turns upon itself, almost completes a circle and ceases. It is marked by the remains of his officers and men and the bodies of his horses. Some of them dotted along the path, others heaped in ravines and upon knolls, where halts appear to have been made."

This description was doubtless due in part to the work of Lieutenant Edward Maguire of the Corps of Engineers, who was on General Terry's staff

5. Ed note: This description refers to Medicine Tail Coulee.
6. Dated "Camp on the Little Bighorn, Montana, June 27th, 1876." [W.O.T.]

and made a map of the battlefield which was afterwards published by the Government.[7]

My second reason is the statements made by the two messengers that Custer dispatched from near the crests of the bluffs, and my inability to believe that he would, after seeing the village close at hand, move his command nearly a mile away from the foe he had so eagerly sought. I am disposed to account for his presence on the ridge by my belief, that after being checked in his attempt to cross the river, and seeing the strength at his front, he believed that by drawing his foes away from the river and village he would render Reno's purpose more successful. And at the same time give Benteen, whom he was expecting every moment, a chance to strike the Indians on their flank or cut in between them and their village. This may be merely an idle thought, but it is one that clings closer the more I read and think about the sad affair.

The story of Custer's Last Fight has ever had a strong and peculiar interest for many people. Poets have sung of it, artists have painted it, and writers have described it, and yet no white man saw it and lived to tell about it. John A. Cockerill, writing for the New York Herald of a visit he paid to the battlefield, says in part; " . . . no pen can describe adequately the formation of the field upon which the fighting took place. The story is plainly told, but no living witness had told it . . . , such is the story of the battle as interpreted by the insensible records. Two hundred and twelve men rode with Custer and two hundred and twelve died fighting. The report might have been written: 'None wounded; none missing; all dead.' "

As I stood on this field, which will ever cradle the memory of Custer and his glorious band, the great brown hills flooded with sunlight and the silence as oppressive as the mystery which surrounds the troopers deaths, I tried to form some idea of the awful sensation which must have come to each of these brave fellows as he realized the horror of the situation; that death awaited every man was evident after the first ten minutes. But my eyes rested on the little white marble sentinels which marked the steady compact advance, and on every hero's cenotaph I seemed to see carved the word

7. See page 72.

"Duty". The requiem of the winds over the graves there can never be sadder than on that golden evening when I turned my back upon this battlefield, at once the most pathetic and most mysterious of all that our sun shines upon.

One of the elements tending to the mysteriousness of Custer's last battle is the fact that within sound of his guns, crouching behind the bluffs, lay over three hundred of his regiment, unmolested until the last of Custer's men had dropped to the ground near the body of their leader, and, strange to say not one of the three hundred although so near had the least suspicion of the actual truth until fifty-six hours afterwards.

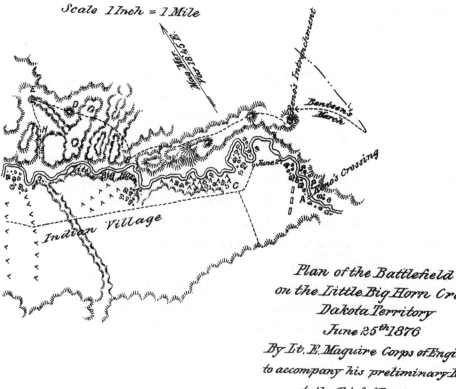

Scale 1 Inch = 1 Mile

Plan of the Battlefield
on the Little Big Horn Creek
Dakota Territory
June 25th 1876
By Lt. E. Maguire Corps of Engineers
to accompany his preliminary Report
to the Chief of Engineers
Dated July 2nd 1876

CHAPTER VIII

Burying Custer's Dead

Soon after five o'clock on the morning of the 28th, the remnant of our Regiment swung into the saddle again and bade farewell to that memorable spot and the scattered graves of our late comrades. It had been our enforced abiding place for two and one half days, and for a great part of the time, it looked as if we had reached the end of our earthly journey. We left it, carrying with us a memory graven deep in our minds of those thrilling scenes when for hours we looked death in the face.

Our errand now was to seek our comrades who had died with Custer, and pay our last respects by a scant and hasty burial. After riding a short distance north, perhaps a little over one and a half miles, we came to an elevation from which a part of the battlefield could be seen. A bleak, dreary place, where, aside from a little coarse grass, nothing grew but an abundance of wild sage and a variety of cactus called prickly pear. Over it there seemed to hang an

> And soft on the rose scented air,
> Hemmed in by the bluff rising high,
> Came the words that to me seemed a prayer
> "I'd lay me down to die."
> —William O. Taylor

atmosphere of sadness and desolation, and little wonder that there was, for from every body on that bloody field but a few hours before had gone forth in vain most anxious looks and prayers for our appearance, which would have meant so much, the salvation of many lives.

The actual field of battle was less than one mile in length and perhaps one half mile in width, the main part being on a ridge that ran nearly parallel with the river and about a mile from it. Most of the bodies were on the slope of the ridge but there were quite a number scattered between the river and the ridge, and how white they looked at a distance, like little mounds of snow. The command now separated, each troop or detachment going over a certain section of the field. Major Reno, who was in command, taking the precaution to send Lieutenant Varnum with his remaining scouts well out on the flanks to guard against any surprise. We had but little in the way of grave digging implements, one spade to a company and that was brought along by the company cook for the purpose of cutting a trench for his fire, so the decent and proper burial of over two hundred bodies was not possible in the limited time at our disposal. The most that could be done was to cover the remains with some branches of sagebrush and scatter a little earth on top, enough to cover their nakedness, a covering that would remain but a few hours at the most when the wind and rain would undo our work, and the wolves whose mournful and ominous howls we had already heard would scatter their bones over the surrounding ground.

*   *   *

"Our errand now was to seek our comrades who had died with Custer, and pay our last respects by a scant and hasty burial."

The first body found was recognized as that of Sergeant Butler of L Troop, [Lieutenant Calhoun's Company] a soldier of proved courage and a veteran of many Indian battles. He was lying near the foot of a hill and about one mile

from where Custer fell and, according to the most reliable map but a little more than a mile in an air line, from Major Reno's position. His body was perfectly nude, and somewhat mutilated but not so badly as some of the others. From some statements made to the writer by an Indian who took part in the battle, the known character of the Sergeant, and the circumstances under which his body was found, it seems altogether probable that he was selected by General Custer soon after the fight began, to make an effort to reach Captain Benteen and hasten his approach, for the situation was becoming serious.

He took the message and started back at a rapid gait and had made quite a little distance before any effort was made by the surprised Indians to stop him. And he might have succeeded in getting away but just as he started to ascend a ridge there appeared on the top a party of Indians coming over from Reno's position. There was no chance for the Sergeant, the party that had started in his pursuit had got his range while the bullets of those in his front were singing about his ears. Escape was impossible. He sprang from his horse, unslung his carbine and the mute testimony of six or eight cartridge shells by the side of his body was sufficient evidence that he had made a gallant fight. *". . . He knew no creed but this, in duty not to falter, with strength that nought could alter to be faithful unto death."*[1]

None of the bodies that I saw had any clothing on whatever and nearly all were mutilated in a terrible, and in some cases most disgusting manner. This was the case all over the field, with very few exceptions, General Custer and Captain Keogh being the only one that I heard of, these two I did not see. That great Russian artist, Tatkeleff,[2] in all his pictures depicting the horrors of war has nothing that equalled the horrible sights presented to our view that morning. Heads crushed to an unrecognizable mass by stone war clubs, arms and legs slit with keen knives, parts of the bodies dismembered, and trunks cut open, and many with arrows left sticking in them.

Nothing whatever of the belonging of man or horse was left on the field that I could see, the squaws had swept it clean. The sagebrush, broken and trampled by the horses and ponies of the contending forces, gave forth a strong odor which, mingled with that of the swollen and fast decomposing remains of horses and men, was sickening in the extreme, and yet so hardened or indifferent were some that I saw men sitting down close by a mangled body and calmly munching their bit of hardtack and bacon.

1. Ed. note: Taylor quotes these lines from the poem "Ad Finem Fideles," by Guy Wetmore Carryl.
2. Ed. note: Taylor is referring to the Russian painter Vogiany Tatkeleff (1813–1880). Tatkeleff's paintings and illustrations were noted for their graphic portrayal of battles of the Crimean War.

Some of the officers went galloping over the field looking at different bodies in the hope of recognizing the three missing Lieutenants; Harrington, Porter, and young "Jimmy" Sturgis. The latter was our Colonel's son, and just out from West Point. But their search was fruitless although they went so far as to feel the palms of one body near me looking for a clue in the way of a soft, uncalloused hand. This body was nude like all the rest and in it were several arrows, two of which I pulled out and brought away.[3] Some of the clothing of young Sturgis, bearing his name was found in the deserted Indian camp. But his body was never found, to be recognized, all statements to the contrary notwithstanding.

Lieutenant Nowlan of I Troop of the Seventh, [Captain Keogh's Company] who was at that time serving on the staff of General Terry, is said to have marked the resting place of many of the officers by driving into the ground a stake, into the head of which had been forced an empty cartridge shell containing the name of the party it was designed to mark. I did not see any such work done nor is the statement verified by First-Sergeant John Ryan, of M Troop, who had charge of the detail that buried General Custer and his brother, Captain Thomas W. Custer. In the burial of these two he was assisted by Privates Harrison Davis, Frank Neeley, and James Seavers all of M Troop. Sergeant Ryan in whose company I served for four years, writes me to the following effect:

"The body of General Custer although perfectly nude was not mutilated.[4] He had been shot in two places, one bullet had entered his body on the right side and passed nearly but not quite through, the second bullet, and undoubtedly the fatal one, passed through his head entering close to the right ear and coming out near the left ear. Under his body was found four or five brass cartridge shells which, with a lock of his hair, was afterwards sent to his widow.

"It was a very difficult matter to identify the body of Captain Tom Custer. He lay some ten or fifteen feet from the General and had been most shockingly mutilated. He had been split down through the center of his body

The officers in the burial party looked for Lieutenant Jimmy Sturgis, "our Colonel's son," writes the author. But his body was never found.

3. Ed note: These arrows were offered at auction in 1995 along with other items collected by William O. Taylor.

4. Ed note: This is not entirely true. Although Custer was not scalped or dismembered, there were several postmortem wounds on his body. In addition to the ones mentioned by Taylor, there were a gash cut in one thigh, a finger digit removed, and an arrow shot into the genital area; also his eardrums had been punctured by a squaw's sewing awl. See Richard Hardorff, *Custer Battle Casualties*, p. 21.

and through the muscles of his arms and thighs, his throat was cut and his head smashed flat. When found he lay on his face. It was not until Sergeant Ryan recalled that when Captain Custer was First Lieutenant of M Troop, in 1873, he had noticed on one arm of the Lieutenant in India ink the letters T.W.C. A careful search was made and although the arm was cut and somewhat blackened, the letters were found, and the body identified. A grave about eighteen inches deep and wide enough for two was dug, and wrapped in some pieces of shelter tents and blankets. The bodies of General Custer and his brother Captain T.W. Custer were laid therein, a little earth placed on them, a basketlike affair torn from an Indian travois was laid upside down over the grave and some stones laid on the edges in the hopes of keeping the wolves from digging it up, and the burial of General Custer was done."

First Sergeant John Ryan (standing) was in charge of the burial detail. This photo has not previously been published.

But one other body was placed in a grave by Sergeant Ryan's party, and that was Lieutenant W.W. Cooke. He was identified by his long black side whiskers, one of which had been taken off for a scalp, for if my recollection is correct the Lieutenant was a little bald. He was the Regimental Adjutant and a long time friend of General Custer.

It has always seemed rather strange to me that the remains of General Custer were not brought along with the wounded and shipped with them on the steamer *Far West*, to Fort Lincoln. There was plenty of salt and strong canvas to wrap the body in, and the steamer was but a few miles away. The Indians carried away many of their dead, why could not the white man do as much for one as distinguished as General Custer? Rightfully or otherwise, there was at the time among the enlisted men at least, a deep feeling of resentment against the General. How far this feeling prevailed among the officers, high and low, is not for me to say. Among the men it was felt then that their comrades had been needlessly sacrificed and their own lives put in jeopardy to further ambition. Later on, when more was known in regard to the number of Indians engaged and certain circumstances connected with the affair, the feeling among the men was greatly changed.

* * *

Having completed our sad duty the command reassembled and started for the ford where the Indians had crossed, intending to go up through the abandoned camping places of the Indians to the camp of General Terry's command which was partly on the ground where Major Reno made his attack. It was not until then that the magnitude of the forces we had engaged dawned upon us. Stretched along the river for miles following its many bends, close up to the bluffs, and then into the prairie was a vast number of lodge sites. Terry's engineer officer counted some eighteen-hundred, so it was reported at the time, and I have never felt like questioning the number. On every hand as we rode along was the evidence of a hasty flight, an immense number of lodge poles, robes, dressed skins, pots, kettles, cups, pans, axes and many other articles among which I saw several decorated box-like receptacles made of rawhide, a kind of traveling trunk I suppose. Also sleeping mats, made of small willow sticks that rolled up like a porch shade. Several war clubs were picked up with the sickening evidence on them of a recent use.

Comanche, with seven wounds on his body, survived the Custer massacre.

* * *

We had gone but a short distance when over toward the river among the bushes was seen a cavalry horse. Upon investigation it proved to be the horse of Captain Keogh, a clay-bank in sorrel color, and named Comanche. He was stripped of all equipment and was a pitiful sight, there being no less than seven wounds on his body, from bullet and arrow, from which the blood had hardly dried. On his mane, where there was no wound was some dried blood which was probably the blood of Captain Keogh. The horse certainly bore a charmed life for he had been wounded once before in an Indian battle while ridden by Captain Keogh. Major Reno gave orders that the horse be secured and taken along with the command, of him more will have to be said later on.

"COMANCHE"

Dead is the steed, Comanche,
Whose Tongue could never tell
The war on the Little Bighorn
When Custer's soldiers fell.
Of Custer's brave three hundred
He only, lived to see
The closing of the combat,
He only, lived to flee!

That night the horse Comanche,
Splashed with Miles Keogh's blood,
Utterly lone and riderless,
Wounded and hungry stood.

Never might living rider
Across his neck draw rein,
Since Keogh's crimson life blood
Had stained his sweeping mane.

by
Evana Reed Tuttle

Soon after we resumed our journey toward the upper end, a cloud of dust was seen in our front and seemed to be rapidly approaching us. What could it

One body "was nude like all the rest and in it were several arrows, two of which I pulled out and brought away."

mean?, was the question everyone asked himself. We were surely quite near to Terry's camp, so it could not be Indians. Major Reno seemed to think otherwise; anyway, he was not ready to take any chances. The command was put into a line of battle, carbines advanced, and scouts dashed forward to investigate, when out of the rising dust rode some fifteen or twenty troopers of the 2nd Cavalry. They were accompanied by some men of the Artillery detachment who had taken the limber[5] and chests off from the caissons and were coming down after some of the abandoned lodge poles to use in making litters and stretchers for the wounded. As they passed us, Major Reno was heard to say to the Lieutenant in charge of the detail, "Young man, you came very near getting a volley that time."

The Major was decidedly nervous about that time, and little wonder perhaps, for who could be otherwise after viewing the sights we had just left. The line of march was again taken up, details spreading out to destroy so far as they could the property left behind by the Indians. On our way we passed a large funeral tepee, in which were some eight of nine dead Indian warriors, fully prepared for burial. They had been killed in the recent battle, and for some reason, unknown at present, were not carried away as many of the dead were. Near

5. Ed. note: The limber is a two-wheeled carriage pulled by a team and used to carry ammunition. Guns are pulled behind the limber.

the tepee lay the bodies of their ponies on which they were to ride to the "Happy Hunting Ground". It has been said that there were two such funeral tepees in the deserted camps; personally I saw but one. Major Reno in his Official Report says, he saw the bodies of eighteen dead Indians.

It was not long before we reached General Terry's camp, which was close by the spot where we first engaged the Indians on the 25th. The Montana Column was a very cheering sight to us after all we had been through and seen. Our wounded and the pack train were close by the other troops and we went into bivouac beside them and started in to complete our preparations to remove the wounded from that ill fated place. Some of our men had been left behind when we went over to the Custer field, and they, with the assistance of the Infantry, had been burying our comrades who fell in Reno's inglorious retreat. They found the bodies scattered from the sides of the bluffs back across the bottom land and in the woods where the flight first began. The stories they told of the condition in which they found Reno's men varied but little from what we told them in regard to Custer's command, stripped clean and most horribly mutilated.

One thing has always seemed rather strange to me and that is how it happened that Charley Reynolds, the guide and scout, Isaiah Dorman, a colored interpreter from Fort Rice, Lieutenant McIntosh, a full blooded Indian, and the three "Ree" Indian Scouts, Bloody-Knife, Bob-tail-Bull and Stab, good shots and well mounted as they were, all men of long and varied experience with Indians and soldiers and familiar with Indian warfare, should have been the first to fall. They were cool, self-reliant, and not bound down with the strict discipline considered necessary for a Soldier. They were, in a sense, free and independent and could fight or run, just as they saw fit. Did they fail to hear Reno's order to retreat? Or was the lust of battle too strong for them to heed the withdrawal of the troops ere the fighting had scarcely begun? How it was we shall never know. One thing is very certain, that several of the men left behind in the woods and elsewhere were too badly wounded to escape and when the bodies were found and buried they bore the evidence of fiendish torture. Isaiah, the Interpreter from Fort Rice, well known to all the

Opposite: A rare composite group portrait of General Custer and his family: Custer (center); brother Captain Thomas W. Custer (top right); brother Boston Custer (bottom right); nephew Autie Reed (bottom left); and brother-in-law Captain James Calhoun—all of whom died on or near Custer Hill.

Sioux along the Missouri River, was shot many times in both legs, and elsewhere, with a small caliber pistol or revolver. This was probably done by the squaws, who were seen to mutilate fallen soldiers by others who were in the bushes hidden.

One of the thoughts that has often come to me was of the mental agonies as well as the physical sufferings endured by many of the seriously wounded. Some were shot while the command was in rapid motion, reeling in the saddle and unable to guide his horse which was, freed of its unsteady burden, dashing away. The last of his comrades are rushing by unheeding, for close in their rear comes the swarming Sioux. The trooper strives to rise but falls back to the ground, his blood spurting forth from the effort, "Oh God, must I die here?" With lightning-like rapidity, many events and scenes of his past life pass through his mind; his dear old mother, who grieved so when he told her he "had joined the Army,"; his brothers and sisters whom he has never thought much about, how dear they seemed just now, and the earth how beautiful it was, even on that dry dusty plain, and the sky, why, it was never so clear and blue before. All these and many more thoughts of a like nature swept over him as the hideously painted and yelling hordes bore down on him. In the front rose one who was coming directly at him, lashing his pony with all his strength in order to count the first "coup". He reaches the side of the wounded soldier and stopping his pony so suddenly fairly lifts it off its feet. A second later and the warrior is on the ground, hatred shining in his eyes. His stone headed war club is raised. The soldier covers his face with his hands breathing a last prayer of "God, have mercy on me". The coup is counted and on the Company Roll, opposite the soldier's name is written later on, "Killed on the Little Bighorn, June 25, 1876."

How the Battle was Fought

The Indians who took a leading part in directing the movements that resulted in Custer's defeat, should be the best authority for what really took place. And yet too much must not be expected of them, for in the tremendous excitement of a battle so close to their village, the hurry of getting their warriors into position to intercept the advancing column, they would not be observing the exact and detailed movements of the enemy. The things that were done on the battlefield after the fight, made the affair a delicate subject for the Indians to discuss. James McLaughlin, for over thirty-eight years, lived among and had official dealings with the Indians, and was for a part of the time the Government Agent at the Standing Rock Reservation. Here he had unrivalled opportunities for learning the Indian story of the great battle on the Little Bighorn, for among the hundreds of late hostiles who had come under his charge were some of the principal chiefs and headmen who participated in the Custer battle. Among them being Sitting Bull, Gall, Crow King, Kill Eagle and Rain-in-the-Face.

The result of Mr. McLaughlin's careful and painstaking investigations he has incorporated in a most valuable and interesting volume under the title of *My Friend the Indian*. From this work I draw what seems to me the most authentic Indian account of the battle. Mr. McLaughlin in speaking of Gall, Crow King and others says: "From these men and many others of less prominence I heard the story of the Custer battle, . . . his last march and stand is therefore gathered from many sources and was told piecemeal."

It may be well now by way of explanation to say that what I gather from Mr. McLaughlin's book is principally in relation to the five troops under General Custer. Whether McLaughlin's theory, as based on the story from the Indians is correct in regard to Custer's first attempt to reach the river being from the ridge, where most of the bodies were found, I am not disposed to admit. That is one of the disputed points, one of the problems that has not yet, and probably never will be, satisfactorily answered.[1]

McLaughlin says:

The morning of the battle the Indians knew where Custer was and what his strength was. When the Sioux first saw the column advancing[2] it was evident to them that Custer intended striking the lower end of the village. They were ignorant of the fact that a considerable portion of the command had been detached. The great mass of the Indians were congregated near the Cheyenne camp where they expected the approaching column to attack, the outermost tepee of which extended to a point almost opposite, or a little below the hill where Custer made his stand. Here Gall had gathered his warriors and when the news was brought to him of the near approach of another enemy, [Reno] he took a large part of his warriors and raced up through the village to the southern end where he turned Reno's flank, drove him with ease across the river and satisfied that no more trouble need be apprehended from that quarter, hurried back to the lower end where a large force was approaching, leaving a few Indians to harass any stragglers and spreading the news through the village that the soldiers attacking at the upper end had all been killed.

Gall said that when he reached the lower end of the village Custer was still some distance off, that his force was advancing irregularly, but the men did not straggle far. Whatever Custer's attitude of mind, he did not waver in his advance.

While his column was still silhouetted against the skyline of the ridge,

1. Ed. note: John S. Gray, *Custer's Last Campaign*, answers many of the questions posed by students of the battle during Taylor's lifetime.
2. In the vicinity of their village.

Crazy Horse with the Cheyennes crossed the river, and under cover of the inner ridge, made their way into the ravine to the north and west of the ridge upon which Custer was advancing. Gall threw many of his people across the river, the Hunkpapas, Minniconjous, Oglalas, Sans Arcs, and Brules crossing in a swarm, some being sheltered from the sight of Custer by the lower ridge, others making their way around the ravine. They were all hidden from the view of the command. Custer swung his troops to the left from the ridge and turned down to the river. As the men rode down into the bottom, the Indians saw that they were apprehensive, but they did not falter and were well down to the river before the Sioux showed themselves on that shore. Of course, the lower end of the village had been in sight occasionally for some time, but it was unlikely that Custer could have known that the Indians had crossed the river to meet him.

With the first shot that was fired the truth undoubtedly dawned upon Custer and his people that they had met a formidable force. The Indians rose up in front of them and in a very considerable number, and went directly to the attack. The soldiers retreated instantly; the ridge behind and the right of the troops. The extension of the elevation they had left to go into bottoms might afford the men a chance to defend themselves. The order to fall back was evidently given without hesitation, though it was apparent to the Indians that Custer was surprised—the movement to the rear was executed with such precision as would be likely in a body confronted by an enemy showing great strength—there was no time for orders, Gall, Crow King, Bear Cap, No Neck, and Kill Eagle, all of whom were in position to see the entire field covered by Custer's force, and who corroborated each other unboastingly, have told me that from the time of the first attack until the last man of Custer's command died on the battlefield, not more time elapsed than would be necessary to

Gall (top); Rain-in-the-Face (bottom)

walk from the spot where the conversation was held at the Standing Rock Agency Office—to Antelope Creek, a mile distant. It might have been a half hour altogether.

Within that period all the defense possible was made, including the movement from the bottom to the height, which was less than a mile. While a considerable body of Indians followed and harassed the men in this movement, another even larger body was sent around the ravine to the rear of the position aimed at Custer; and when the Cavalrymen had attained the position from which the commander evidently thought he might hold the Indians, in the ultimate hope of succor from Reno or Benteen. The elevation was surrounded to the west and north, while a considerable mass of the Sioux were advancing on what might be called the front of Custer's position. In this retreat from the river . . . a dozen or more troopers were killed; their bodies were found at intervals along the line of the backward movement, as indicated by the marble slabs which mark the spot where each dead trooper was found.

When Custer reached the elevation, Keogh's and Calhoun's troops were halted and dismounted by command, or by the necessities of the action, and the horses left in the ravine. This gave the troops the left of the force when Custer had proceeded along the ridge and turned to face the Indians in sight on the ground covered in the retreat. Between Custer and Keogh, Smith's troop was extended in skirmish formation, a fact evidenced by the disposition of the bodies. Captain Tom Custer's and Captain Yates' troops, who fell in the group with General Custer, were farther along toward where the ridge ran out in a declivity, which could not be easily negotiated by horsemen, and which made the command comparatively safe from attack in that direction. This, then was the position at the finish. The line was not a long one, and the men were thickest at about the point where Custer fell.

A rare photo of Crow-King (sitting, left) with Low-Dog (sitting, right). The two other men are unidentified.

While the troops were getting into this position, they were fighting continuously, but the onslaught of the Indians did not take on its deathly and irresistible form until Gall, in carrying his men around the ravine to the north and east of the position, struck the cavalry horses, probably those of Keogh's and Calhoun's commands. The shouting and shooting incident to the stampeding of the horses was the signal for the attack on the troops from three sides of the ridge.

The Indians rose up out of the ravine and rode at the devoted column. [At this time Custer was well out to the right of the command.] The stand of the troopers was of the briefest duration. When Gall gave the signal, the Indians rose up out of the ravines, the Cheyennes led by Crazy Horse, the Hunkpapas, the Blackfeet, the latter few in number, the Minniconjous, with Lame Deer and Hump in the van. The Oglalas, with Big Road, the Sans Arcs and the Brules. They came straight at the ridge, riding fiercely and swiftly, stayed by nothing, a red tide of death; and almost without pause they rode over the field, and the desperate shooting of the white men did not halt them for a moment. When the tide had passed, Custer and his men were reckoned with the dead. There was neither time nor opportunity for defense; personal gallantry and the desperate occasion may have given birth to heroes in the moment, but they died in the instant of their birth, and Custer's last stand was a bloody page in history.

Out to the north and east these men had sought safety only to be shot down. The rest of the command, with the exception of Sergeant Butler, whose body was found over toward Reno Hill, died as they stood.

It seems a fitting time and place for the statement made by Captain Charles King, formerly of the Fifth Cavalry, who was with a Battalion of his regiment that passed over the Custer battlefield in the summer of 1877.

"With this battalion were a number of Sioux scouts, mainly Brule's and Oglalas, who had as hostiles, taken a part in the battle of the Little Bighorn. In telling the story of the fight, the scouts said that one man, an officer they thought, managed to break through their circle and galloped madly eastward. Five warriors started in pursuit, but the soldier was well mounted and his splendid horse gained on all but one Hunkpapa who hung to the chase. At last, when even this one was ready to draw rein and let him go, the hunted cavalryman glanced over his shoulder, fancied himself nearly overtaken, and placing the muzzle of his revolver at his ear, sent his own bullet through his brain."

His skeleton was pointed out to the officers of the Fifth Cavalry by one of the pursuers, and so it was discovered for the first time. Was it Lieutenant Harrington?, or Sturgis? Neither of those bodies were found to be recognized, at the time of the burial, June 28th.

Returning to the Indians' story of the battle, McLaughlin says:

The Indians participating in that affair have always asserted and still maintain with decided positiveness that the fight was of short duration and the Indian loss insignificant; that the attack of the overwhelming number of Indians, enthused by their easy victory over Reno, was of such whirlwind force that the small groups of soldiers did not check the rush of their wild charge. The Indians claim that many of the soldiers were killed without being shot, some who were mounted being pulled off their horse and clubbed to death with stone-headed war clubs, which many of the Indians carried in addition to the Winchesters.

Gall told me that he would have gone at once to the attack of Reno when the fight on Custer Hill was over, if he could have controlled his warriors. As well try to stem the flood of the mighty Missouri, he said, as to hold the wildly excited hundreds who dashed about on the ridge among the bodies of the slain. Some scores of horses that had lately been ridden by the white man, the most valuable booty for an Indian, were galloping about the country. These were spoil for the warriors, and they turned their attention at once to their capture.

As the men left the field the women and boys came on. The women carried stone clubs, little hatchets and knives, and the ferocity with which they attacked the bodies of the dead makes a horrid detail of the affair that has been told more than once. Even the Indian boys walked or rode about over the field shooting into the bodies of the slain.

As soon as possible after the fight Gall led his people away from the field and rode up the river to the position which had been held in absolute safety by Reno, while Custer's command was being wiped out of existence. I have been assured by many credible people among the Sioux that for at least an hour there was not an Indian left in front of Reno's position; and that he might have marched out uninterrupted.[3] Custer's force was destroyed about three o'clock, and it was after four when Gall got his warriors started up the river to attack the Reno position.

And this is the story of the battle of the Little Bighorn. For many moons the story of that day, recounted by the warriors who had a part in it, bolstered the fading hopes of the Indians, who in scattered and starving bands sought to avoid the unevitable capitulation to the white soldiers who pursued them from that day in June until the last of them surrendered. For years after the Indians had laid down their arms it was talked about around the camp fires of the bands that had nothing left of the old life but the memory of the day when the last power of the Sioux nation was arrayed in its great strength and in successful opposition to the march of the white man.

The fighting force of the Indians in this battle, including boys over fourteen, was, according to Mr. McLaughlin, "not less than twenty-five hundred, and the population of the camps altogether, about 10,000." Frederic Remington, who from long experience in depicting the varied life of Indians and soldiers in the far West, has been unsurpassed in fidelity to actual and minute detail, a fidelity born of long and close association with the subjects which he loved to portray, wrote and illustrated a sketch for the Cosmopolitan Magazine, with the title: *The Way Of An Indian.* A part of this sketch incidently dealt with the battle on the Little Bighorn. His pen drawing of the Indian charge was most

3. Not without leaving the wounded, which was not an option.

realistic, as I well know from meeting with the same Indians, on the same day, and in very much the same manner. I therefore feel that this brief extract will be a most fitting supplement to, and round out the story told to Mr. McLaughlin by the Indians.

At the ford of the river they made the water foam, and far side muddy with their drip. They were grotesque demons, streaked and daubed, on their many colored ponies. Rifles clashed, pony whips cracked, horses snorted and blew, while their riders emitted the wild yelps which they had learned from the wolves. Back from the hills came their scouts sailing like hawks, scarcely seeming to touch the earth as they flew along. The Pony soldiers are coming—they are over the hill, they cried. The crowded warriors circled out and rode more slowly as the chiefs marshaled them. The view of the hill in front was half cut by the right bank of the coulee up which they were going, when they felt their hearts quicken. One, two, a half dozen, and then the soldiers of the Great Father broke in a flood across the ridge, galloping steadily in column, their yellow flags snapping. The "Fire-Eater"[4] turned and gave the long yell and was answered by the demon chorus—all whipping along. The whole valley answered in kind, the rifles began to pop, a bugle rang on the hill, once, twice, and the pony soldiers were on their knees, their front a blinding flash, with the blue smoke rolling down upon the Indians or hurried hither and thither by the vagrant winds. Several of the Indians reeled on their ponies or waved from side to side, or clung desperately to their pony's necks, sliding slowly to the ground as life left them. Relentless whips drove the maddened charge into the pall of smoke, and the fighting men saw everything dimly or not at all. The rushing Red Lodges passed through the line of the blue soldiers, stumbling over them and striking downwards with their war clubs. Dozens of riderless troop horses mingled with them, rushing aimlessly and tripping on dangling rope and reins. Soon they were going down the other side of the hill and out of the smoke; not all, for some had been left behind. Galloping slowly, the red warriors crowded their cartridges into their guns

4. Ed. note: Name of the principal character in Mr. Remington's story.

while over their heads poured the bullets of the soldiers who, in the smoke, could no longer be seen. On all sides swarmed the rushing warriors mixed inextricably with riderless troop horses mad with terror. As the clouds of Indians circled the hill, the smoke blew slowly away from a portion of it, revealing the kneeling soldiers. Seeing them the Fire Eater swerved his pony and followed by his band, charged into and over the line. The whole whirling mass of horsemen followed them, the scene was now a mass of confusion which continued for some time, until no more soldiers could be found. As the tumult quieted and the smoke gave back, they all seemed to be dead. Around and about the warriors were hacking and using their knives, but the enemy had been wiped out. Horses lay kicking and struggling, or sat on their haunches like dogs with blood flowing from their nostrils.

It may be observed that in the preceding sketch of Mr. McLaughlin's, there is but a scant mention of some of the other Chiefs and Head men who were arrayed against Custer in this memorable battle, among them being Sitting Bull, Two Moons and Crazy Horse. One reason for this may be the fact that many of the Indians were from, and afterwards returned to other Agencies than Standing Rock, and so were beyond Mr. McLaughlin's observations. In fact, he does not credit Sitting Bull with having anything to do with the generalship and disposition of the combined Indian forces that gathered from many quarters, in that little far away valley fought a desperate and successful battle, and then moved their huge camp away in the very eyes of another advancing body of soldiers.

It is, I think, generally conceded by most writers that so far as generalship is concerned, Crazy Horse was easily the most prominent among the chiefs who confronted Custer. He had fought two battles with the soldiers earlier in the season, the second one occurring on the seventeenth of June, when he stopped the advance of General Crook's force of about twelve hundred men, and forced him to retire to his base of supplies and call for reinforcements. Captain Charles King of the Fifth Cavalry says that, "While Gall, Lame Deer, and others were probably leading spirits in the battle, the man who more than all other won the admiration of his fellows for skill and daring on that bloody day, was the warrior Crazy Horse."

Among the chiefs and Head-men who took a more or less prominent part in that last great battle between the white and Red men there are a few whom it might be well, for history's sake, to recall by name at least. Of the four whom I consider the most noted, Sitting Bull, Gall, Crazy Horse and Rain-in-the-Face, more will be found farther on, but at this point I want to make a brief mention of several of the lesser lights.

Two Moons, a Cheyenne chief, was engaged in the battle and of all the leaders, survived the longest for he was still living in 1913, at his home on the Reservation at Lame Deer, Montana, not many miles from that historic field where he battled and Custer fell. Hamlin Garland, the author, had an interview with him a few years ago and says, "He was a tall old man, big chested, erect, and martial of bearing, his smiling face was broadly benignant, and his manners were courteous and manly. All that was strong and fine and distinctive in the Cheyenne character came out in the old man's talk. He seemed the leader, and the thoughtful man he really is patient under injustice, courteous even to his enemies."

Lame Deer, whose tragic death when about to surrender, is so much to be deplored.[5] "Dull Knife" that dauntless Cheyenne whose camp was attacked and destroyed in the winter of 1876, and his people dispersed. "American Horse" was killed near Slim Buttes while in his way to the Agency. Many others might be named but time and space forbids.

5. Ed. note: On May 7, 1877, near Muddy Creek, Montana, Lame Deer and Iron Star, while in the act of surrendering to General Nelson Miles, were startled by the abrupt approach of an armed scout. Fearing betrayal, they seized their weapons and were quickly dispatched by the troops nearby.

[C H A P T E R   X]

The Montana Column

After our sad return from Custer's bloody field, as already stated, we went into camp near General Terry's command. The expedition had so far proved a most disastrous failure. The enemy had fled, our supplies were few, the loss of life had been great and the large number of wounded that needed attention made it necessary to get back to our base of supplies, send the wounded home and reorganize the command.

Before we start on our march back to the Yellowstone it might be well to say a few words in regard to our rescuing comrades, giving a brief sketch of their earlier experiences and describing as far as possible, in a limited space, their march in an effort to act in conjunction with General Custer in an attack on the hostile Indians. This part of our story is in the main drawn from journals kept by Lieutenant James H. Bradley, Chief of Scouts, Lieutenant E.J. McClernand, Engineer Officer, the Official Report of General Gibbon, and a most interesting sketch by Lieutenant Charles F. Roe, then, in 1876, an officer of the Second Cavalry, and later a Major General of the N.Y.N.G. to all of whom, due acknowledgements are hereby given.

In pursuance to General Terry's order as Commander of Department of Dakota, Colonel John Gibbon of the Seventh Infantry, commanding the Disrict of Montana, was in the latter part of February 1876, directed to prepare for the field all the troops which could be spared from his disrict and move as soon as able down the valley of the Yellowstone. It was not intended that these troops should attack the Indians, unless a very favorable opportunity offered itself. But its main duty was to guard the left bank of the Yellowstone, and if possible prevent the Indians from crossing. This command consisted of six Companies of the 7th Infantry, four Troops of the 2nd Cavalry, and about 25 Crow scouts. It was under the direct command of Colonel John Gibbon, (better known as "General".)

The infantry portion took the field on the Seventeenth of March, 1876, marching from Fort Shaw to Fort Ellis. They reached the latter Post on the 28th of March. Here they were joined by the Cavalry under Major Brisbin. The Infantry left Fort Ellis on the 30th of March and the Cavalry on the 1st of April, heading for the Yellowstone river down which they were to scout, and if possible confine the Indians to the south side of the river until the arrival of General Terry's command.

Of the long hard marches through the snow and mud, the fording of rivers of cold water, living for weeks on half rations, and the other attendant hardships but little has ever been written.[1] But a more hardy, uncomplaining and ever-ready body of men never wore our Army uniform. In the six months of their campaigning they marched nearly 2,500 miles, and, as may easily be imagined, were a pretty seedy looking lot of men, but full of grit and large of heart, willing to take their chances against the Indians, either individually or collectively as the following incidents will show.

While encamped on the Yellowstone near Old Fort Pease, General Gibbon desired to learn if possible the whereabouts of the hostile Indians, and for this purpose he dispatched on the 24th of April two companies of the Second Cavalry, numbering in all about 80 men. This little force, under the command of Captain Ball, and Lieutenant C. F. Roe, left camp about noon, crossed to the south side of the Yellowstone and then proceeded up the Bighorn Valley to the ruins of Old Fort Smith where they arrived on the 27th. Their marches were largely in the evening or night and very early in the morning to avoid being seen.

Leaving Old Fort Smith the next day they moved in a north easterly direction and on the 29th struck the Little Bighorn at the point where Custer found the great Indian village a few weeks later. It bore evidence then of

1. Ed. note: For a well-written account of the Montana Column, see Edgar I. Stewart, *Custer's Luck.*

being a favorite camping place of the Sioux and liable to be again. One of the Crow scouts with Captain Ball's command, taking abandoned hard bread box and a piece of charcoal, covered it with a lot of drawings, which he said, "would tell the Sioux that we meant to clear them out." And then sticking a handful of green grass in the cracks, he added, "And this will tell them that we are going to do it this summer." A taunt and prophecy that was fulfilled, but not that summer.

Lieutenant McClernand, who as acting Engineer Officer for General Gibbon accompanied this scouting party and to whose valuable report we are greatly indebted, says of this incident, "It is a little strange, considering the hundreds of miles we have marched over, that this taunt should have been left almost on the very spot where the one desperate fight of the campaign took place."

Following down the Little Bighorn a few miles they crossed the river and bore off to the right and after marching about five miles across the divide, struck one of the tributaries of Tullock's Fork, which they found to be dry. Following it down they soon find another little creek in which the buffalo had just wallowed. As it was the only water to be had they went into camp for the night. Continuing down Tullock's Fork and the Bighorn they arrived at General Gibbon's camp on the Yellowstone on the first of May, having marched 178 miles through the very heart of the Indian country and without seeing any recent signs of the enemy. And yet the very next night the Sioux crept up to the camp and stole the ponies of the Crow scouts.

And once more there comes to mind a notable example of heroism. Scarcely two weeks after Custer's defeat, three of Gibbon's stout-hearted Infantry men volunteered to carry a dispatch from General Terry on the Yellowstone to General Crook whose exact whereabouts was not known, but was supposed to be about thirty or forty miles south of where Custer fell, and in the same general direction that the victorious Indians had taken. These men had seen Custer's dead scattered about over the plain, mangled beyond recognition, yet they did not hesitate to take their lives in their hands and ride out in that same unknown, and dangerous country, seeking a command over a hundred miles away. Of such material was the Montana Column.

Scouting down the Yellowstone which was closely watched and followed by scouting parties of the Indians who succeeded in stealing the ponies of the Crow scouts, and later killing three of the command who had strayed too far away, General Gibbon's force came in contact with General Terry's column near the mouth of the Rosebud. Here a conference was held and on the 21st of June General Gibbon started back up the Yellowstone, headed for a point on the Little Bighorn to meet General Custer's command on the 26th of June and possibly the long-sought after hostiles. The Steamer *Far West* with General Terry and staff went later.

Lieutenant Bradley, chief of scouts for General Gibbon, kept a journal on this campaign and a part of it was published in vol II, *Contributions to the Historical Society of Montana*, 1896. Quoting from his journal, which is as good authority as can be found, we learn that Gibbon's command arrived about opposite the mouth of the Bighorn on the afternoon of the 23rd. The Far West arrived early the next day, June 24th. After drawing eight days rations and fitted with a small pack train, five companies of the 7th Infantry, and four troops of the 2nd Cavalry, were ferried across the river by the *Far West*, all being over about four o'clock. They at once started up the valley of the Bighorn, coming to Tullock's Fork, a small stream emptying into the Bighorn on the east side and about five miles from its mouth. They marched up this valley for about a mile and went into camp at 6 p.m.

On the fatal 25th of June they broke camp at 5:30 a.m., marched up Tullock's fork about two miles, then turned to the right. Lieutenant Bradley had meanwhile continued up the stream for some nine miles, in the hope of getting into communication with Custer, or some of his scouts,[2] but was recalled and joined the main command. He made another scout of eight miles but not seeing anything of the Little Bighorn returned once more to the command at 6:30, just as the Infantry went into camp in the valley of the Bighorn, having marched some 23 miles.[3] General Terry with the Cavalry and Gatling guns pushed on about ten miles farther, being accompanied by

2. Note by General C. F. Roe.
3. Over very rough country under a very hot sun, and without any water for a great part of the way. [General Roe]

WITH CUSTER ON THE LITTLE BIGHORN

Lieutenant Bradley and his detachment of mounted Infantry and Crow scouts.

It commenced to rain about nine o'clock and was as dark as a pocket, so much so that the men had to travel in single file and were then scarcely able to see the second man in front of them. To add to their troubles the Gatling guns got into a mud hole and were lost for some time but finally made their appearance. The column that had been waiting and searching for them resumed the march, which had involved the command in a labyrinth of bald hills and deep precipitous ravines. At length, after they entrusted themselves to the guidance of one of the oldest of their Crow scouts who soon conducted them to a good camping place by an easy route, at about midnight the weary troopers unsaddled and lay down on the wet ground for a short rest.

Monday, the 26th, Major Brisbin, who was in command of the Cavalry battalion roused Lieutenant Bradley at daylight and ordered him out on a scout at once but Bradley did not get away until 4 o'clock a.m. When, having advanced about three miles, he discovered heavy smoke rising in his front and apparently some fifteen or twenty miles away. At the same time he came upon the fresh tracks of four ponies. He took up the trail at once and found that it led to the Bighorn, less than two miles away where the party had crossed, leaving behind a horse and several articles of personal equipment which, on examination, proved to belong to some of the Crows that had been furnished to General Custer. On the opposite side of the river three men were seen about two miles away. After some signaling with blankets and smoke, they were induced to come down to the bank of the river and talk with Little Face and one or two others of the Crow scouts that Bradley had sent down.

Lieutenant Bradley says,

Presently our Indians turned back and as they came, shouted out at the top of their voices a doleful series of cries and wails that the interpreter explained was "a song of mourning for the dead." When they came up, shedding copious tears and appearing pictures of misery, it was evident that the occasion was of no common sort. Little Face in particular wept with a bitterness of anguish such as I have rarely seen. At last he composed himself and told his story in a shaking voice, broken with frequent sobs. As he proceeded, the Crows one by one broke off from the group of listeners and going aside a little distance sat down alone, weeping and chanting that dreadful mourning song. They were the first listeners to the horrid story of the Custer massacre, and outside of the relatives and personal friends of the fallen, there were none of this whole horrified nation to whom the tidings brought greater grief.

Lieutenant Bradley goes on:

The three men over the river[4] were in truth a portion of the six scouts furnished to General Custer from my detachment, and this is the story they told to Little Face.

Custer had followed the Indian trail and yesterday had struck the village on the Little-Bighorn, the Sioux letting him get close to the village and then sallying forth in great numbers to meet him, defeating his command, and destroying all but a small portion who had been driven into the hills and surrounded by the Sioux, where the Crows had left them fighting desperately. The corpses of Custer's men were strewn all over the country, and it was probable that every last one was killed, as it was impossible for the party who had taken refuge in the hills to hold out long. For the Sioux immensely outnumbered them and were attacking them in dense masses on all sides. Of the six Crows who had gone with Custer, two,—White Swan and Half Yellow Face,—were killed, and another—Curley—was missing and probably also killed.

It was my duty to report the matter to General Terry. And I rode back where I saw the head of the column appearing over the ridge a couple of miles away. I narrated to the General the ghostly details as I received them from Little Face. For a moment there were blank faces and silent tongues

4. Ed. note: Their names were Goes Ahead, White-Man-Runs-Him, and Hairy Moccasin.

in the group, but presently the voice of doubt was raised and the story sneered at by some of the staff officers. General Terry took no part in the criticism but sat on his horse silent and thoughtful. After a few moments he cried, "Forward," and once more the column was in motion.

(This incident, it is well to remember, took place near the mouth of the Little Bighorn). General Roe says, "at its juncture with the Bighorn," and the time about 5:30 or 6 o'clock a.m. June 26th. It might be added that all of the Crow scouts, with their interpreter, deserted the command right after hearing the news of Custer's overthrow.

Lieutenant Bradley continues:

The Infantry who had remained in camp twelve miles back, joined the Cavalry toward noon. The whole command then advanced together into the valley of the Little Bighorn. The heavy smoke was now continually in view. After passing up the valley a few miles, the column halted about three o'clock p.m. to allow the men to rest and make coffee. During the rest period, two white scouts, Bostwick and Taylor, were sent forward to try to get into communication with Custer or some of his command. At five o'clock General Terry started his command once more, the Infantry on the left, near the river, and the Cavalry on the right, the general officers and their staffs in front between the two lines.

They had marched but a few miles when a man was seen approaching as rapidly as his horse could travel. It proved to be the scout Bostwick who, as soon as he got within hearing said excitedly, "You have been looking for Indians all summer, you will find all you want there!", pointing to the bench land about six miles away. Lieutenant Roe, with his troop was ordered up on the bench land as advance guard and from the right flank of his position he could see a strong skirmish line of Indians. And in their rear, some distance away, was a large body of mounted men, some three or four hundred. Out of this body rose, to all intents and purposes, a troop of Cavalry marching by twos with a guidon flying, the riders dressed in dark clothes. Soon, another supposed troop marched forward. A Sergeant and two men of Lieutenant Roe's troop was sent forward but as soon as they came within range of the reinforced skirmish line, were met with a sharp volley. The Indians had dressed themselves with the uniforms of Custer's men and were trying to mislead the advancing soldiers by the adoption of some military formations. Sending a report to General Terry, Lieutenant Roe soon received a message to stay where he was until dark and then come back into camp, which he did about eight o'clock.

While this was taking place on the right of the column Lieutenant Bradley's detachment was acting as advance guard on the left near the river. It was drawing near a grove into which he had seen squad after squad of Indians riding with the apparent intention of resisting at that point the further advance of the troops. But just as he reached within a quarter of a mile of the timber, the whole command was halted. It was then twilight and the troops, weary and worn, went into camp. Bradley says, "at nine, o'clock" No fires were allowed and the men lay upon their arms.

Lieutenant Bradley goes on:

From subsequent examination of the grove that was before me I am convinced that there were not less than a thousand of these ambushed savages, with plenty more to cooperate with them. Not only would they have easily defeated the Cavalry, but they would have given our whole command a desperate fight had we advanced another mile. Their village was retreating, and they were there to cover it, and it was only for lack of an hour or two of daylight that we did not come upon them in force and prove once more the terrific gallantry with which they can fight under such an incitement as the salvation of their all.

Lieutenant Bradley's notes of this campaign, taken on the march and in camp, had been compiled during his leisure moments after the return of his command up to June 27th, 1876. It stops abruptly at the very outskirts of Little Bighorn's fatal field. It is evident that at this point he was called to enter upon the expedition against the Nez Perces in 1877, where he was killed in an engagement with Chief Joseph's band on the 9th of August 1877. [5]

---

5. Note by W.E.S. in James H. Bradley, "Journal of the Sioux Campaign of 1876."

Chapter XI

The Crow Scouts Story.

The situation, as the Montana Column went into camp that night was one well calculated to give General Terry much cause for anxiety. The rumor that he had received in the morning of Custer's terrible defeat, he could not wholly accept. He had planed to meet General Custer on the 26th of June, somewhere on the Little-Big-Horn, he was there, but, where was Custer. The two men, Taylor and Bostwick whom Terry had sent ahead in an endevour to open communication with Custer had been unable to make any headway, for they soon ran into a strong force of Indians and had a very narrow escape with their lives. At the same time the progress of his advance guard under Lieut Roe had been disputed by a large force, which at first sight had the appearence in dress and action of at least two full Troops of Covalry, but which soon proved to be Indians, dressed in the clothing taken from Custer's men and who were acting as a rear guard to cover the retreat of their village

Terry had been expecting a courier from Custer and for that very purpose had given to him one George Herendeen, a man who was familiar with the country, but nothing had been heard from him. Were all the carefully made plans to come to naught, the morrow would show. Taking up the story from Lieut McClernands report we

The Crow Scout's Story

The situation, as the Montana Column went into camp that night, was one well calculated to give General Terry much cause for anxiety. The rumor that he had received in the morning of Custer's terrible defeat, he could not wholly accept. He had planned to meet General Custer on the 26th of June, somewhere on the Little Bighorn. He was there, but where was Custer? The two scouts, Taylor and Bostwick, whom Terry had sent ahead in an endeavor to open communication with Custer, had been unable to make any headway, for they soon ran into a strong force of Indians and had a very narrow escape with their lives. At the same time the progress of his advance guard under Lieutenant Roe had been disputed by a large force, which at first sight had the appearance in dress and action of at least two full Troops of Cavalry, but which soon proved to be Indians dressed in the clothing taken from Custer's men and who were acting as a rear guard to cover the retreat of their village.

Terry had been expecting a courier from Custer and for that very purpose had given to him one George Herendeen,[1] a man who was familiar with the country, but nothing had been heard from him. Were all the carefully made plans to come to naught, the morrow would show.

Taking up the story from Lieutenant McClernand's Report we find the following:

June 27th. The night passed away quietly making an early start. We go but a short way (General Gibbon says, "about three miles".) when two tepees

---

1. See Herendeen's account of the battle in Appendix I.

are seen through the timber. Crossing a narrow sandstone point, we see just in front of us where a very large village was yesterday. Our scouts reported only a few scattered horsemen in sight on the distant hills and we continue to move more rapidly forward, still uncertain as to the fate of Custer's command. Captain Ball's Troop about a mile in advance.

While passing through the Indian camp, a report reached us from our scouts in the hills to the north of the river that a large number of bodies of white men had been discovered. Shortly afterwards Lieutenant Bradley came in with the information that he had "counted 194 bodies of dead soldiers," and while he had never seen General Custer, he believed from the likeness of one of the bodies to Custer's photograph, that the General was among the slain. What Lieutenant Roe saw yesterday looking like buffaloes lying down were dead comrades and their horses. All doubt that a serious disaster had befallen General Custer's command now vanished, and the march was continued under the uncertainty as to whether we were going to rescue the survivors or to battle with the enemy who had annihilated him. The two tepees were found to contain the dead bodies of Indians. Many lodge poles were still standing, and the quality of property such as Buffalo robes, dried meat, blankets, and all kinds of camp utensils scattered about, testified to the hasty departure of the Indians.

At length we caught sight of a number of animals congregated upon the slope of a distant hill and on a point nearer to us three horsemen were evidently watching us. After Captain Ball's company had passed them, these cautiously approached us, our troops being in plain sight and marching in two columns abreast of each other. At length, convinced that we were friends, they came forward more rapidly and proved to be Lieutenants Wallace and Hare of the Seventh Cavalry. They informed us that the Seventh Cavalry has been cut to pieces, and the remnant under Major Reno were entrenched on the bluffs near by. They eagerly inquired if we knew anything as to General Custer's whereabouts and are told what Lieutenant Bradley had just discovered. Communication was now opened with Major Reno, and my command was placed in camp at the foot of the bluffs that had been in a state of siege for nearly two days, having marched 8³/₄ miles.

Lieutenant Charles F. Roe, who was in command of F Troop of the Second Cavalry on this campaign and later became a Major-General of the New York Militia, wrote a very interesting story of the Custer Fight which he delivered, in 1904, before the National Guard Convention at Albany, New York. This story was afterwards [March 1910] published in *The Castle*, a magazine devoted to the interests of the 22nd Regiment N.G.N.Y. A copy was kindly sent to me by the author.

Speaking of the advance of the Montana Column General Roe says in part: "We found in the Indian village a white man's head with a lariat tied to it, which had been dragged around the village until the head was pulled off the body." (This may have been one of the men of G Troop whose horse became unmanageable in Reno's fight in the bottom and ran away with him right into the Indian lines.) And again, in speaking of the mutilation of Captain Tom Custer's body, General Roe says: "His heart was cut out, and in the village was found a man's heart with a lariat attached to it, possibly Captain Custer's. In front of my Troop after we went into camp, there was a dead body lying, naked, and the features hammered into jelly. This body was soon after recognized as that of Lieutenant McIntosh by his brother-in-law Lieutenant Gibson, of H Troop, who was shown a gutta-percha sleeve button picked up near the corpse, both officers having been given the same kind of sleeve buttons by their wives just before leaving Fort Lincoln. The body of Mitch Bouyer, the half-breed scout, was found on Custer's field and not far from the river. It also was very badly mutilated."

It has been quite generally accepted as fact that out of all those who rode with Custer that fatal afternoon, but one escaped after the first shot was fired and that was a Crow Indian scout named Curley. Whether the whole story that this man has told us is true or not, I am of course unable to state, positively, but I have always had my doubts as to certain parts of it. Nevertheless a few facts in regard to our scouts, and the story of Curley as well should be of interest and this is a good place for it.

When the Seventh Cavalry started up the Rosebud on the 22nd of June it was accompanied by the majority of the Ree Scouts who had come with us from Fort Lincoln and also by six Crow scouts and a half breed interpreter, the latter being named Mitch Bouyer. These men were selected from General Gibbon's command by Lieutenant Bradley on account of their familiarity with the country over which we expected to travel. Lieutenant Bradley says in his journal that, "they were his best men, and that as a guide, Mitch Bouyer was the very best that the country affords." The Crows had, upon their introduction to General Custer, declared their willingness to "eat mule, rather than to abandon a trail." Now let us see how they made good.

Soon after our arrival at the mouth of the Little Bighorn with the wounded we learned from some of the boat guard that Curley, a Crow Scout who had been with Custer, had escaped the general slaughter and had made his appearance at the steamer *Far West* on the 27th and, by signs, told of Custer's defeat.

This story is best retold by J.M. Hanson in a most interesting book entitled *The Conquest of the Missouri*, a volume dealing largely with the life of Grant Marsh, the Captain of the steamer *Far West*, from whom Mr. Hanson obtained the greater part of the story that Curley told. Quoting from this book we learn that,

> Between 10 and 11 o'clock a.m. of the 27th [of June] the steamer *Far West* lay tied up to a little island in the Bighorn river just about opposite the mouth of the Little Bighorn. The water teemed with pike, salmon and catfish, and Captain Marsh, his Engineer Foulk, and Pilot Campbell, together with Captain Baker and Lieutenant Carlin of the boat guard, strolled out from the boat and engaged in the general pastime of fishing. The smoke seen along the southern horizon for the past two days has disappeared and the opinion was that Custer and Terry had met the enemy and routed

them, and that there was no fear of their being surprised where they were. While idly discussing the matter, the bushes on the mainland opposite them parted and a mounted Indian warrior, naked, save for a breech clout, pulled up his sweating pony at the brink of the water and held up his carbine in sign of peace. Scrutinizing him closely, the officers soon recognized him as Curley, one of the Crow scouts who had gone with Custer.

As soon as he came aboard he gave way to the most violent demonstrations of grief, groaning and crying. When he had, to some extent, regained his self control, the question arose how to communicate with him, for no one on board could understand the Crow language while he spoke no English. After a while, by the use of a paper and pencil, which he had been shown how to use, he made a rude diagram. First a circle and then, outside of it, another. Between the inner and outer circle he made numerous dots, repeating as he did so, "Sioux! Sioux!" Then he filled the inner circle with similar dots, which, from his words and actions they understood him to mean were soldiers. Then by pantomime he made his observers realize that they were receiving the first news of a great battle in which many soldiers had been surrounded, slain and scalped by the Sioux.

By the use of their limited knowledge of the sign language they were able in the course of hours, to observe some details. According to Curley, General Custer was killed and all who went into action with him, excepting the Crow himself. He declared that he had been in the thick of the fight, but seeing that the battle must end in the annihilation of the soldiers he picked up two blankets and going to Custer implored him to throw one of the blankets over his head and attempt under Curley's guidance to escape. But Custer refused to go and told Curley to escape if he could. Curley, putting a blanket over his head and watching for an opportunity, worked his way to the outer edge of the Sioux hordes and then rode northward into the valley of the Little Bighorn. Using great caution he made his way to the mouth of the stream where he arrived 48 hours after that battle although the distance was only eleven miles.

* * *

The previously mentioned General C.F. Roe [then a lieutenant], in his story of "The Custer Fight," says that, "Curley, the Crow was afterwards under his command as a scout, and through an interpreter, gave his account of what occurred with Custer's command. How correct this one of the many versions that Curley had given is, it is impossible to say, but from his knowledge, and experience with the subject Lieutenant Roe was well fitted to obtain a near approach to the truth.

"Curley says they went along through the Badlands out of sight of the river as much as possible, when they came to a little creek called 'Green Grass Creek' [Reno's Creek]. Running down into the Little Bighorn, to the left on the river, was a high cut bank, some seventy five feet high. Bouyer, Curley, and two or three of the Crows went down, got on that point and looked over into the village. The Cavalry came down the creek by twos. Custer halted the command, went down to the bluff and looked at the village, then went back to the command, which moved down the creek to where it empties into the Little Bighorn.

"After the head of the column reached the river, Curley saw a man on a gray horse with stripes on his arm, meaning a Sergeant, ride into the river, evidently to see if he could find a ford. At that moment the Indians opened fire on the column. The head of the column turned back from the river, Custer apparently having made up his mind that they could not cross there, and as they moved down the river they motioned to the other troops to break out, so that practically they broke out almost in echelon. Curley ran back and joined the pack train, which was in the rear on Ash Creek." [No reference has ever been made, that I have seen by anyone connected with the pack train, or the guard (B Troop) accompanying it, of any Crow scouts coming back to them.]

* * *

Since those stories were first told by the Crow he has repeated them many times, and with more or less variations and additions. To be known as the only survivor of the "Custer Massacre," gave him an importance in the eyes of newspaper men and others that seldom falls to the lot of an Indian. And Curley, or his interpreters, whoever they happened to be, was not slow to take advantage of it; and for a proper consideration, a very thrilling article could be had. Without desiring to cast any reflections on the truthfulness of the Crow, I do feel that many of the details of his stories are the creations of his imagination. The three Crows whom Bradley ran down have also indulged themselves in varied and fanciful stories of the part they claim to have taken in the battle, and some of their stories have become embodied in historical literature. The gist of the first story told by Curley, as well as that of the three Crows told to Lieutenant Bradley, I believe to be reasonably true. That Mitch Bouyer, the guide and interpreter, Curley, and two or three more, of the six Crow scouts rode with Custer's battalion after the division of the Regiment there is no doubt, but that any of them, with the exception of Mitch Bouyer stayed after the first few shots were fired is altogether doubtful, and is not believed by any officer or man who was present on that day.

Oscar Wright, who was for a number of years the Superintendent of the National Cemetery at Custer's Battlefield, which is quite close to the Crow Indian Reservation, in a letter to the writer, under date of May 1, 1910, speaks of these six Crow scouts:

"I had quite a talk recently with Mr. Stossell, [a photographer at Crow Agency for many years] in regard to Curley and the other Crow scouts. Mr. Stossell said that on their return to the column after discovering the location of the Sioux camp, the scouts told General Custer that there were too many Indians for him to whip with his command. General Custer would not believe them and said 'If they were afraid, to go back.' Mitch Bouyer replied that, 'they were not afraid, and would go with him.' "

Mr. Wright continues: "We all believe that Curley, and the three who met General Terry's command were not in any part of the battle, either with Custer or Reno."

General Godfrey, in his story of the fight, says:

"On the evening of June 22nd I happened to pass the bivouac of the

Indian scouts, Mitch Boyer, Bloody-Knife, Half-Yellow-Face and others were having a 'talk'. I observed them for a few moments when Bouyer turned toward me, apparently at the suggestion of Half-Yellow-Face and said, 'Have you ever fought against these Sioux?' 'Yes', I replied. Then he asked, 'Well, how many do you expect to find?' I answered, 'Between 1000, and 1500.' 'Well, do you think we can whip that many?', 'Oh yes, I guess so.' After he had interpreted our conversation he said to me with a great deal of emphasis, 'Well, I can tell you we are going to have a —— big fight.'"

And further on Godfrey says: "On the morning of the 25th, just before setting out on the march, I went to General Custer's bivouac; the General, Bloody Knife, and several 'Ree' scouts and a half-breed interpreter were having a 'talk', after the Indian fashion. The General's face wore a serious expression and he was apparently abstracted. The scouts were doing the talking and seemed nervous and disturbed.[2] Finally, Bloody Knife made a remark that recalled the General from his reverie, and he asked in his usual quick, brusque manner, 'What's that he says?' The interpreter replied. 'He says we'll find enough Sioux to keep us fighting two or three days.' The General smiled and remarked 'I guess we will get through them in one day.' "

Colonel Varnum, who as a Lieutenant, was in command of the scouts under General Custer in this campaign, informed me in 1911, that, "On the division of the regiment, about 12 o'clock June 25th, Custer took four of the six Crows with him." These four were Curley, White-Man-Runs-Him, Hairy Moccasin, and Goes Ahead. Now if these scouts, at a distance of fifteen or twenty miles from the hostile village, were satisfied, from the evidence of the trail and late camping places, that the enemy was in too great a force for our whole regiment to attack, what must have been their condition of mind when a few hours later they saw, less than a mile away, that vast camp of the Sioux. And then, looking, saw the small force of soldiers (about two hundred) with whom they were riding. It is not strange that they decided to leave as soon as possible.

Northeast of the battlefield and not very far away lay the foothills of the Little Wolf, or Rosebud Mountains. From their summit there might be

2. Ed. note: This was immediately after the Crow scouts had located the Indian camp.

obtained by the keen eyed Indians, a fair, and safe view of the ridge where Custer fell. And it was doubtless to these hills that the Crow scouts fled when they saw the overwhelming hordes of Sioux warriors riding out to encircle and destroy Custer's little band. From the shelter of these hills they could work their way northward until they felt it safe to turn to the left and strike for the Bighorn, and then their Agency. This is but a theory, perhaps a mistaken one. But where was Curley for nearly 45 hours after the battle began, and the other three for, about 16?

Chapter XII

Back on old Camping Grounds.

Before leaving this scene of the greatest Indian victory known in our history I must mention one more incident in connection therewith. Late in the Afternoon of the 25th, and again on the 26th while we were besieged on the bluffs, two or three smoke signals were plainly seen for a long time on the hills west of the Indian Village. They did not attract much attention from our command as no one seemed to understand their meaning, to us they were simply "Indian signals," of some kind. They were, in appearance, very high and straight pillars of smoke, varying at times in depth or intensity of color, sometimes being quite light and then again very dark. It was not until long afterwards that the true import of these signals became known to us. Little we thought at the time that the news of our battle was being sent to all points of the compass, whereever there was a Sioux Camp, or warrior, and, incredible though it may seem it is doubtless a fact that the defeat of a large body of soldiers on the Greasy-Grass, (Little Big Horn) was known to the Agency Indians on the Missouri river and elsewhere, many days before the whites had any inkling of Custer's defeat. It was more than nine full days from the afternoon of June 25th before the first news was heard by the outside world through the arrival at Bismarck on the morning of July 5th of the Steamer Far-West, bringing back the wounded and the news of Custer's last battle. That something serious

Back on old
Camping Grounds

Before leaving this scene of the greatest Indian victory known in our history, I must mention one more incident in connection therewith. Late in the afternoon of the 25th, and again on the 26th while we were besieged on the bluffs, two or three smoke signals were plainly seen for a long time on the hills west of the Indian village. They did not attract much attention from our command as no one seemed to understand their meaning. To us they were simply "Indian signals" of some kind. They were, in appearance, very high and straight pillars of smoke, varying at times in depth or intensity of color, sometimes being quite light and then again very dark. It was not until long afterwards that the true import of these signals became known to us.

Little we thought at the time that news of our battle was being sent to all points of the compass, wherever there was a Sioux camp, or warrior. Incredible though it may seem, it is doubtless a fact that the defeat of a large body of soldiers on the Greasy-Grass, [Little Bighorn] was known to the Agency Indians on the Missouri river and elsewhere many days before the whites had any inkling of Custer's defeat. It was more than nine full days from the afternoon of June 25th before the first news was heard by the outside world through the arrival at Bismarck on the morning of July 5th of the steamer *Far West*, bringing back the wounded and the news of Custer's last battle. That something serious had happened to the military was suspected by many at Fort Lincoln for several days before the arrival of the *Far West*. The Indian scouts attached to the Post betrayed by their actions that they had heard some important news. The same thing was noticed to even a greater degree at Standing Rock Agency, some sixty miles below Fort Lincoln.

Lieutenant J.B. Rodman, of the 20th Infantry, who as Regimental Adjutant was stationed at Fort Snelling, Minnesota, near St. Paul, and some 435 miles from Bismarck, was informed on the third day of July [just about the hour the *Far West* started from the mouth of the Bighorn[1] with our wounded] by an old Sioux Indian whom the Lieutenant had often befriended—"that a great battle had taken place between the Indians and the soldiers on the 'Greasy Grass', (Little Bighorn) that the battle lasted for two days, and many soldiers and chiefs were killed, and more soldiers were coming. That the Indians where he lived (Mendota) all knew about it and were dancing and singing."

The story was not credited in the least by the Lieutenant who flatly called his informer a dreamer, or a liar. But on Wednesday morning, forty eight hours afterwards, the Steamer *Far West* arrived at Bismarck, Dakota, and the first news of the disaster was flashed over the wires to the people of the States. A few hours later when the news reached Fort Snelling, the old Indian was sent for and told to repeat his story, and was asked this question, "How on earth could all this have reached you Indians at Mendota, forty eight hours before the telegraph could tell us?" The old blind Indian replied, "Indians use Indian runners, mirror flash, fire arrows, fire and smoke, Indians tell that story faster than the fastest pony."

In September 1880, an outbreak occurred at Fort Reno [Indian Territory] sixty miles from the location where Colonel Dodge was stationed, yet his Indian scouts knew of it and so informed him before he heard of it by the telegraph line between the two places. That this Indian method of sending news may be more readily understood, I will quote a few lines from *Smoke Signals* in the Ethnology Report of 1879–80, page 537.

1. This was 710 miles from Bismarck.

The highest elevations of land are selected as stations from which signals with smoke are made—they can be seen at a distance of from twenty to fifty miles, by varying the number of columns of smoke different meanings are conveyed. Building a small fire which is not allowed to blaze, they put an armful of partially green grass or weeds over the fire, as if to smother it, a dense white smoke is created, which ordinarily will ascend in a continuous vertical column for hundreds of feet. By covering and uncovering it at proper intervals, a succession of elongated egg shaped puffs of smoke are kept ascending toward the sky in the most regular manner. These bead-like columns of smoke are visible on the level plain fifty miles distant.

*   *   *

It was late in the afternoon of the 28th, not far from 6:30 p.m. that the united commands, the Montana Column and the surviving part of the Seventh Cavalry, began their return march. The transportation of fifty-two wounded men was quite a serious problem as neither of the commands had started out with stretchers or any other means for carrying the wounded. Possibly they did not expect that there would be any. At first, litters made out of abandoned lodge poles on which were stretched blankets, with four men as carriers were tried. But fifty or sixty feet was all the carriers could walk without resting. The poor wounded fellows could not stand being let down to the ground so often. Starting with four men to a litter, in a little while we had eight, so that four men could put the poles on their shoulders and as they got tired they were relieved by the four men who walked alongside of them. Thus we had eight times fifty, or the greater part of the infantry command carrying the wounded Cavalrymen.

Although the march was continued until nearly midnight, we only made a little over four miles, and then went into camp, on the river, near what was the north end of the village. Early on the 29th Lieutenant G.C. Doane of the Second Cavalry was called upon to continue the construction of more serviceable litters. Cottonwood poles, about twenty feet long, were cut, dead horses were skinned and from the rawhide, strips were cut and laced between the center of the poles to make a bed. A mule was put in between the shafts at one end and another at the rear, the poles being supported by the rigging of the packsaddles; an infantry soldier led each mule. This work took nearly all day but proved very satisfactory. The wounded were put in their rude litters and went along as comfortable as possible.

A second start was made at 6 p.m. with the expectation of making a short march, but the litters worked so admirable as to call forth the most unbounded commendation in praise of the skill and energy displayed by Lieutenant Doane.

After making a few miles, word was received by two couriers from Grant Marsh, the Captain of the *Far West*, that the steamer was waiting for us at the mouth of the Little Bighorn, General Terry therefore decided to continue the march with the view of placing the wounded in comfort and rest as soon as possible.

After following the valley for several miles, the command turned to the left and soon gained an elevated plateau. On this plateau there was found a great quantity of large cactus, known as prickly pear, and as the night was dark and stormy it proved very annoying to man and horse for it could not well be avoided. The way from the end of the plateau was very rough but Captain Marsh very thoughtfully ordered out his entire crew to build fires at frequent intervals along the way and lighted the troops forward.

About one o'clock in the morning the head of the column, looming weirdly through the darkness in the flickering firelight, approached the boat. Captain Marsh had caused a portion of the deck to be thickly covered with grass, and over it had spread a lot of tent flies, making the whole like an immense mattress and in a short time, the fifty-two stricken men were placed on board and with them Keogh's horse, Comanche. The men were laid in rows on the grass covered deck and Dr. Williams, and H.R. Porter set about examining and dressing their wounds. Soon afterwards, General Terry and Staff, with Major Brisbin, though weary, travel stained, and utterly depressed by the results of the past few days, went on board also, and just as it began to grow light the steamer started for the Yellowstone.

June 30th, General Gibbon, being left in command of the troops, crossed the Little Bighorn to the north side about five o'clock a.m. and went into a pretty camp among large cottonwood trees for a short but much needed rest. The next day, starting about five o'clock a.m., we made but 20 miles and camped again on the Bighorn. July 2nd we resumed the march, and arriving at the Yellowstone, were ferried across by the *Far West* that had been waiting for us for that purpose and we went into camp on the north side, a short distance below the mouth of the Bighorn river.

*   *   *

Our new camp on the Yellowstone was not altogether an unfamiliar place to many of us, for in August 1873 we had spent several days in the same locality, part of the time in an unsuccessful attempt to ford the river and continue on the trail of a large war party of Sioux whom we had been following for several days. In this party led by Sitting Bull, Gall, and Black Moon, was the afterwards notorious Rain-in-the-Face, who, a few days before, (Aug 4th) had killed two men who had straggled a little way from the command. Being unable to cross the river after the Indians, they, very obligingly came over to our side and gave us a battle which might have been longer and more disastrous had it not been for the arrival of General Stanley and his infantry command with two field pieces. As it was, our loss was slight, four killed and four wounded as I remember it.

The dead Soldiers were buried at twilight and all in one grave, and the burial was conducted with all the impressive ceremonies incidental to a soldier's funeral. The troops parading with reversed arms and forming a hollow square in the center of which was the grave. The band playing the Dead March. A brief service was read, a volley fired over the grave, and then "Taps" was blown. It was quite a solemn affair and two or three men fainted during the ceremony, the heat and excitement of the day probably having something to do with that. After the burial, a picket line was stretched across the grave and a troop of horses tied there for the night. This was done to obliterate all signs of a burial so that the Indians could not find the bodies and scalp them.

Two years later, a party of citizens established a trading post at this point, called Fort Pease. In less than a year they lost eight of their number through the attacks of the Indians. I often wonder if the bodies of these twelve men still rest in their shallow, unknown graves, or have their bones been turned up by the plow or pick of the first settlers.

While lying in this camp Captain Lewis Thompson, of the Second Cavalry, committed suicide on the 19th of July by shooting himself with a revolver. No reason was known for the rash act, unless as it was believed by many and so stated in camp at the time, that the hardships of the campaign, and the horrors of the Custer battlefield had, as it undoubtedly had done to others, unsettled his mind. It was not an uncommon thing to happen on that summer's campaign. Private Crowley, of A Troop, and another private, of D Troop, whose name I have forgotten, both of the Seventh Cavalry however, were sent home on that account from this camp. Two soldiers of Lieutenant Sibley's scouting party from General Crook's command went completely crazy after being chased by the Indians soon after the battle and not so very far from where it occurred. Captain Charles King of the Fifth Cavalry in his book, *Campaigning with Crook*, speaking of the hardships of the campaign of 1876, says that "the Custer massacre had been responsible for the unmanning of just three members of the Fifth Cavalry." (And yet that Regiment did not come out until late in July, and had no part in the Custer campaign.)

Soon after the junction of the commands of General Terry and Crook, four officers and twenty-one men who had broken down under the severity of the campaigns were examined by Surgeon and pronounced as unfit for field service, and ordered home on the *Far West*, several of them being more or less insane. "Rounding up the hostile", or in other words seeking to deprive a strange and brave people of their birthright and all they held dear, was not altogether a picnic. The hardships and privations endured by the Regular army soldiers, have been so fittingly described in those two most interesting volumes, *War Path and Bivouac* by John F. Finerty, and *On the Border with Crook* by John G. Bourke, that there is nothing left for me to say on that subject.

We had scarcely got settled down in the camp, when a petition circulated among the enlisted men, and addressed to the "Powers that be", asking for the appointment of Major Reno to be Lieutenant Colonel of Seventh Cavalry in place of Lieutenant Colonel Custer, deceased. Giving, as a reason for an unheard-of action, for he was far down on the list, that "By his bravery and skill he had saved the rest of the regiment from Custer's fate", or words to that effect. This petition, it was believed by most of the men, to have had inspiration and origin at Reno's headquarters from whence it was circulated by the Chief Trumpeter. Although it was signed by most of us, it was done so rather than to give any offense by a refusal. As Sergeant McDermott remarked "It was a d—d humbug, but what's the odds?" It seemed to be the opinion of many, quietly expressed later on, that the whole affair was simply intended as an aid in putting Reno in a better light and to be used, perhaps, in case of a Court of Inquiry or Court Martial.[2]

* * *

We remained on the Yellowstone until the 27th of July when the entire outfit started down the river, and on the 29th, arrived opposite the mouth of the Rosebud where we went into camp. A few days later reinforcements consisting of twelve companies of infantry arrived. On the 7th of August, the whole command was ferried over the river, and early the next day started up the valley of the Rosebud on another search for the hostiles. On the 10th they met General Crook's column coming down the river, the two commands effecting a junction at a point which but a few days before had been the camping place of a very large force of Indians, who well aware the near approach of the two columns, had quietly slipped away between them, separating into several parties and going in various directions. The two commands of Terry and Crook again took up the trails and followed them here and there for several weeks but fruitlessly, so far as the original plan of the campaign was concerned. Finally, along in September the commands gave up the chase, and started for their respective stations, the Seventh Cavalry going to Fort Lincoln, but with a different appearance they presented from that on the 17th of May.

2. See Robert Utley, ed., *The Reno Court of Inquiry*.

When the Regiment came back all the guns and swords were black.
And the uniforms had faded into gray,
And the faces of the men who marched through the streets again
Looked like faces of the dead who lost their way.
For the dead who lost their way could not look more gaunt and gray.
Oh the sorrow and the anguish of the sight.
Oh the weary lagging feet, out of step to drums that beat
When the Regiment came marching from the fight.

Ella W. Wilcox

The Seventh had returned, with the exception of those who were taking their last, long sleep, "with Custer, on the Little Bighorn".

On the evening of June 24, 1876 the U.S. Seventh Cavalry, under the command of General Custer, while following the trail of the hostile Indians, went into bivouac in a most beautiful spot on the Rosebud River in Montana. It was the night before the memorable battle of the 'Little Bighorn.' The Indian scouts had returned, and reported the location of the hostile village, and the officers of the command had been called together for instruction. After the party broke up some of the younger officers gathered in a little group and began to sing. The songs were mostly of a tender and homelike nature, given with much feeling, and as I thought, verging on sadness; they ended with the Doxology. The officers bade each other good night and retired to their companies for a few hours rest. Before sunset of the next day, the battle had been fought, and every one of the singers lay stark and cold on Custer's last battlefield. Lying quite near the group of singers, it was my fortune to hear the songs, the location, circumstances and the aftermath, making a deep and lasting impression on my mind and resulted in the following poem. [See page 122.]

Opposite: This photo of Taylor's discharge, January 1877, which he received after serving out his five years' duty with the 7th Cavalry.

ON THE ROSEBUD

It was June on the banks of the Rosebud
"The Seventh" in bivouac lay,
Hard and fast on the trail of the hostiles
We had ridden that long summer day,

And now in a bluff hidden shelter
We had stopped for a time to take breath
Knowing well ere the sun set the morrow
We should ride in the shadow of death.

For our scouts, all excited and restless
Had returned bringing with them a clue
That beyond the Divide, in a valley,
Lay the camps of the war-gathered Sioux

And all who followed our Custer
Knew well that a stranger to fear,
He would strike, be the odds ere so many
As soon as their camps did appear.

As the twilight grew deeper and darkened
And all was so quiet and fair,
An Officer group near the river
With songs woke the still night air,

"Little footsteps soft and gentle, the goodbye at the door,"
While "Maxwelton Braes are Bonnie,"

comes to me o'er and o'er,
Songs of home and the Fireside,
Songs of love tender and sweet,
And the last one, was it meant for a prayer
Sent up to the great mercy seat?
"Praise God from whom all blessings flow,
Praise him all creatures here below,
Praise him above ye Heavenly Host,
Praise Father, Son and Holy Ghost."

Good-night, "Good-night" and parting thus,
Each sought his soldier bed,
A blanket spread upon the ground,
The bright stars overhead,
And the next day, on the Big Horn,
Midst savage shout and cry,
As the sun was slowly sinking,
They "laid them down to die."

Years have passed, and the bones of the singers
Are mingled in the dust of the plain,
Yet often at twilight I fancy
I hear once more that refrain,
"I'd lay me down to die."

And green, ever green in my memory
Are the songs I heard that night
By our Officers sung on the Rosebud
In the twilight before the fight.

—William O. Taylor

After Thoughts

"DOWN FORGOTTEN TRAILS
TO THE CAMPS OF LONG AGO"

After completing the foregoing chapters I found that there were a number of things that might have been included, but as they were not, I have purposed to bring them all together under the title above, believing that they are of sufficient interest and value to be preserved in this work. Some of the items are the result of much patient investigation and research, and represent the writing of many letters to comrades who were knowing of facts but who have since "passed over the Great Divide".

Under the heading of A Red Quartet, I offer some views entertained by several qualified persons in regard to some of the most noted Sioux Indians engaged in the Battle of the Little Bighorn. And in the said views I most heartily concur.

WILLIAM O. TAYLOR

A Red Quartet

THEY LOVED THEIR LAND, BROAD SET
BETWEEN THE SEAS

Of all the Indians who attained notoriety through connection with the Battle of the Little Bighorn the names of Sitting Bull, Gall, Crazy Horse and Rain-in-the-Face, stand out most prominent, and a few words concerning these four may not come amiss.

SITTING BULL
Ta-tan-kah-yo-tan-kah

Sitting Bull was a full blooded Sioux of the Hunkapapa band. This name, also written Uncapapa, means "Those who dwell by themselves". According to one of his alleged statements, Sitting Bull was a son of He Topa [Four Horns.] Although Mr. James McLaughlin says that his father was Sitting Bull senior, and bestowed his own name on his son, then called Jumping Badger, for some war-like deed. Be that as it may, he was born about 1837, in the val-

SITTING BULL.

Sitting Bull circa 1880. The author states, "In all the years of my service on the frontier where he was supposed to roam, I never heard of any act of cruelty or barbarism being charged against him."

ley of the Great River, some distance southwest of Standing Rock Agency.

Of his life prior to 1876 very little is known. He was not a Chief but what is called by the white man, "a Medicine man". His great indisposition to accept the encroachments of the whites on the land of his fathers in direct violation of solemn treaty, caused him to shun them as much as possible, and he frequented the unsettled wilds of Dakota and eastern Montana.

After the defeat of Custer, the Indian forces separated, many of them returning to the Agencies, but Sitting Bull's band, after several encounters with General Nelson A. Miles' command, escaped into Canada where they remained until 1881. When finding himself deserted by many of his prominent followers and his people destitute and nearly starving, Sitting Bull returned to the United States and surrendered to General Miles. He was sent to Standing Rock Agency where in 1890 he became involved in the Messiah, or Ghost Dance Craze, and during an attempt made to arrest him at his home on Grand River by a party of Indian Policemen, was shot by one of the force, December 15, 1890. Two of his sons, Blackbird and Crowfoot, were killed with him. He is said to have had two wives, and nine daughters, one daughter bearing the name of Standing Holy.

In all the years of my service on the frontier where he was supposed to roam, I never heard of any act of cruelty or barbarism being charged against him, but as I never, knowingly met him face to face, I will merely record a few words concerning him from those who have.

W.H.H. Murray, a well known writer, commonly called "Adirondack Murray", after hearing of his death, paid an eloquent tribute to Sitting Bull in the *New York World*. He said: "I knew this man; knew him in his relation to his high office among his people and in his elements as a man. This man Sitting Bull was a prophet, not war chief, to his people. What was a misnomer, to us in our ignorance of facts and things, to the Red Man . . . was a rank above all ranks won or bestowed by the tribe; an office . . . connected with, and symbolic of the highest truths and deepest mysteries of their religion. Hence by virtue of his office he was the counselor of chiefs, . . . the oracle of mysteries and of knowledge hidden from the mass; even from the chiefs, . . . Such was Sitting Bull as to his office, as interpreted from a standpoint of knowledge of the religion, the traditions and superstitions of his people. That he was faithful to his high office all knew, . . . that leaf of laurel none can deny to his fame, . . . I met him often; I studied him closely . . . and I knew him well, and this I say of him, he was a Sioux of the Sioux, . . . in him his race, in physique, in manners, in virtues, in faults stood incarnate, . . . His word once given was a true bond. . . . He was a born diplomat, . . . there was no surface to him, he was the embodiment of depths, . . . But why say more of this man? Have we not as a people fixed the brutal maxim in our language, 'That the only good Indian is a dead Indian.' We laugh at the saying now, but the cheeks of our descendants will redden with shame when they read the coarse brutality of our wit. I read that the great Sioux was dead, that he was set upon in the midst of his family, . . . and killed . . . and I said, understanding the conditions and circumstances better than some, 'That is murder.' . . . I ask that the spot where this great character was buried be carefully marked . . . for as the Lord liveth . . . a monument shall be builded on that spot before many years—if I live—inscribed to the memory of the last great Prophet of the Sioux, and of the noble characteristics of the red race, whose virtues like his own were many, and whose fate was pathetic."

F.A. Rinehart, in his *Prints of American Indians*, says of Sitting-Bull: "Owing to the annihilation of General Custer and his command by the Indians under the old chief in the battle of the Little Bighorn in 1876, it seems impossible to find any account of his deeds which is not colored by prejudice, if not gravely misrepresented. He was a valiant and brave leader, he was feared by his foes and loved and admired by his people. All white men were the enemies of the Indians, and Sitting Bull's logic would permit no other conclusion. He believed that in transactions with them, the Indians would be cheated and swindled. He wanted nothing to do with them, he had no land to sell them at any time, and never gave an emissary of the Government the least encouragement. He was consistent in his refusals to deal with the Government as represented by the Military or the Agents, and the charges of deceit and treachery so often made have no foundation in fact."

John F. Finerty in his book *War Path and Bivouac* says: "I don't care what anyone says about Sitting Bull not having been a warrior, if not the sword, he had, at least, the magic sway of a Mohammed over the rude war tribes that engirdled him. Everybody talks of Sitting Bull, and whether he be a figurehead or an idea, or an incomprehensible mystery, his old time influence was undoubted, his very name was potent. He was the Rhoderick Dhu of his wild and war like race, and when he fell, the Sioux confederation fell with him."[1]

CRAZY HORSE
Tashunca-uitco

Crazy Horse was a son of the chief Crazy Horse, of the Ogalala[2] band of the Sioux. His mother was a sister of the famous Spotted Tail, and he was a brother in law of the noted Red Cloud. Crazy Horse had, during the last two years of his life, a bitter experience with the white man. Roaming over territory which had been reserved for the Indian only, he was ordered to come into the Agency before the first day of February, 1876, or he would be regarded as hostile and turned over to the military. This order he neglected, or was unable to obey, and accordingly on the seventeenth of February Colonel Reynolds, with six or eight Troops of Cavalry, attacked his camp on the Powder River. The Indians, taken by surprise, fled to the hills, leaving the camps and all their property in the hands of the troops who at once proceeded to destroy it and all its contents by fire.

1. Finerty, *War-Path and Bivouac*, p. 335.
2. Dakota for "Wanderers in the Mountains."

The night preceding and following the attack was so cold that the soldiers were not allowed to sleep for fear of the consequences, the thermometer failing to register the intensity of the cold. The weather was so bad the troops were ordered back to their stations.

On the seventeenth of June, the village of Crazy Horse then located on the upper Rosebud was again attacked by a large force under General Crook. This time without any success, for after several hours fighting Crook was obliged to fall back to his base of supplies. A few days later Crazy Horse moved his camp over to the Little Bighorn and joined forces with Sitting Bull. Here on the 25th of June, eight days after the battle with Crook, Crazy Horse was once more engaged in conflict with the soldiers, being attacked in his camp by the Seventh Cavalry under General Custer. The result was a great disaster for the whites, a result to which the bravery and skill of Crazy Horse was undoubtedly a great contribution.

After the battle of the Little Bighorn he was successful in eluding the troops of Generals Terry and Crook and retreated with Sitting Bull to the north side of the Yellowstone. He remained a so called hostile until the Spring of 1877. Many of his band had never been on a reservation nor did they want to go, but the several encounters with the troops and a realization that the government meant to subject them at any cost, aided by the persuasions of Red Cloud, who went out on a mission to them, finally induced them to come in. On the 6th of May, 1877, Crazy Horse and his band of about twelve hundred people, of whom over three hundred were warriors, surrendered to General Crook at Camp Robinson, near Red Cloud Agency.

Reservation life was altogether too tame for Crazy Horse and he longed for the freedom of going where and when he pleased; permission even to go out and hunt buffalo was denied him and rumors reached him that the Sioux were to be transferred to the Indian Territory. Indeed, some of the Cheyennes had already been taken there and Crazy Horse began to cherish plans that he might slip out of the Agency and, far away in the north resume the old way of life. But his purpose was detected and in the Fall of 1877 it was decided to arrest and place him in confinement at Omaha. His arrest was effected by some friendly Indians under leadership of Little-Big-Man, a former Lieutenant of Crazy Horse, and John F. Finerty says, "one of the greatest rascals unhung." While being taken to the guardhouse at Red Cloud Agency, he resisted and in the melee was cut in the lower part of the abdomen either by a knife in the hands of Little-Big-Man, or by the bayonet of a soldier, both claiming the distinction. He was taken to the hospital where he died about midnight September 5th, 1877, hurling curses at the palefaces and the Sioux renegades, "The bravest of all the brave hostiles," so John F. Finerty calls him.

Lieutenant John G. Bourke of Crook's staff, who was present at the surrender of Crazy Horse, says in his very interesting Book, *On the Border with Crook*, "I saw before me a man who looked quite young, not over thirty years old, five feet eight inches high, lithe and sinewy, with a scar in the face. The expression of his countenance was one of quiet dignity, but morose, fogged, tenacious, and melancholy. He behaved with stolidity, like a man who realized he had to give in to fate, but would do so as sullenly as possible. . . . All Indians gave him a high reputation for courage and generosity. In advancing upon an enemy, none of his warriors were allowed to pass him. He had made hundreds of friends by his charity toward the poor, as it was a point of honor with him never to keep anything for himself, excepting weapons of war. I never heard an Indian mention his name save in terms of respect. In the Custer massacre, the attack by Reno had at first caused a panic among women and children, and some of the warriors, started to flee, but Crazy Horse, throwing away his rifle, brained one of the incoming soldiers with his stone war-club and jumped upon his horse, . . . when taken to the hospital his father and Touch-the-Clouds remained with him till he died, and when his breath ceased, the Chief laid his hand on Crazy Horse's breast and said: 'It is good; he has looked for death, and it has come.'"

Crazy Horse was one of the great soldiers of his day and generation. He never could be the friend of the whites, because he was too bold and warlike in his nature. As the grave of Custer marked the high water mark of

Sioux supremacy in the trans-Missouri region, so the grave of Crazy Horse, a plain fence of pine slabs, marked the ebb.

GALL
Pi-zi

Gall, who was for a long time one of Sitting Bull's most prominent followers, was born about 1838 or 1840, and like his leader was of the Hunkpapa tribe of Sioux, whose hunting grounds ranged from the Grand River on the south to the Yellowstone on the north. Like many of the famous red men of his time he was not a hereditary chief but came into prominence on account of his fitness to lead and his commanding ability as a warrior. He was associated with Red Cloud in the Fort Phil Kearney massacre of 1866 and for many years was active in opposing the advance of the white people into the territory set aside for the Indians only. In an assault on Fort Buford he was desperately wounded in the breast by a bayonet and left for dead, but an old medicine woman noted for her skill in healing wounds succeeded in stopping the flow of blood and restoring him to health. He is said to have been with Crazy Horse in the battle of the Rosebud, June 17th, and ably seconded that great Indian General in his charge against General Crook's troops.

In the battle of the Little Bighorn, with his head chief, Black Moon, he led the charge against Reno and shared with Crazy Horse the honor of defeating the soldiers under General Custer. Retiring into Canada with Sitting Bull, he remained there but a few years, then with many of his people he returned early in 1881 and surrendered to General Miles at Poplar River, Montana and was soon after sent to the Standing Rock Agency where he arrived about June 1st. From this time until his death he adhered to the promise to remain at peace with the Government.

In his personal appearance he was a most striking figure, standing six feet high and weighing over 200 pounds, and for an Indian, is said to have had an unusually pleasing and dignified manner, and from the veneration with which his memory is held by his people, he must have been possessed of unusual kindness of heart. He died at his home on Oak Creek near Standing Rock in 1896. He left no sons and but one daughter.

RAIN-IN-THE-FACE
Itiomagju

Rain-in-the-Face was a full blooded Sioux of the Hunkpapa band. Various causes have been ascribed for his name but the one which seems most probable is that when a child he was left outside of the tepee for a short time thoroughly wrapped up except his face. A sudden shower came up and before his mother reached him his face was dripping with water, and his father at once bestowed on him the name aforesaid. He was the youngest of six brothers, the others bearing the names of Bears-Face, Red-Thunder, Iron-Horn, Little-Bear, and Shave-Head. When he grew to manhood he was in the habit of associating himself with the bands of Sitting Bull, Gall, and Black Moon. In 1873 he was hanging close to the column of General Stanley's Expedition (guarding the Surveyors of the N-P.R.R.) which was moving along the north bank of the Yellowstone river. The expedition, which included the Seventh Cavalry, had, about the fourth of August, reached a point nearly opposite the mouth of Tongue River, not far from the present site of Miles City, when Rain-in-the-Face observed two stragglers a short distance from the column, a Mr. Baliran, the sutler, and Dr. John Honsinger, Veterinary Surgeon, both attached to the Seventh Cavalry. These men were unarmed and Rain-in-the-Face dispatched them both and escaped unnoticed. The next year he came back to Standing Rock Agency on a visit, and while there was heard to boast of his deed. A report was sent to General Custer at Fort Lincoln, about sixty miles away, this was in the winter of 1874, and the General at once ordered

Captain Yates and Lieutenant T.W. Custer with a strong detail to proceed to Standing Rock and if possible, effect the arrest of Rain-in-the-Face. This was done in the trader's store, Lieutenant Custer seized the man from behind and held him until he was disarmed, when done he was bound and placed in the guard house. While in confinement at Fort Lincoln General Custer had him brought to his house and held several interviews with him and finally succeeded in getting a confession of the whole story. During this time Rain-in-the-Face was treated very kindly by the General who allowed his brother Iron Horn and others to visit him, and even spent several hours in the Guardhouse with the prisoner. Before any legal steps could be taken however, Rain-in-the-Face escaped from the guardhouse one night in April, 1875, and rejoined the hostiles from whence he is said to have sent a message of threat and defiance to Lieutenant Tom Custer.

In the following year, at the battle of the Little Bighorn, the wheel of fortune favored "Rain-in-the-Face" and, according to his own story, told at Coney Island, New York in August 1894, while under the influence of liquor, gave forth a narrative that was gruesome in the extreme, but which bore every evidence of being the truth.

He admitted recognizing Lieutenant Custer in the battle and said that the Lieutenant [then a Captain] knew him, and when he got near enough "he shot him, . . . cut his heart . . . bit a piece out of it and spit it in his face," and then, wounded as he was in two places, got on his pony and rode off shaking the heart of gallant Tom Custer in his hand. In corroboration of this, I may say that a human heart, attached to a lariat, was picked up in the deserted camp by one of General Gibbon's men as they marched to Reno's relief two days after the battle. Tom Custer's body when found showed a most terrible mutilation, the worst of any on that dreadful field. Longfellow in his poem *The Revenge of Rain-in-the-Face*, written very soon after the battle, made the not very unnatural mistake of confusing the two Custers, or, used poetic license in the last line of the seventh verse.

After his return from Canada in 1881, Rain-in-the-Face settled down at Standing Rock and in the course of time became one of the Indian police force. In 1886 he expressed a great desire to go to school at Hampton, but his age excluded him. This desire led to the poem *On The Big Horn,* by John G. Whittier. Rain-in-the-Face died at Standing Rock Agency, Sept 12, 1905 aged about 62 years. ("He left no issue.")

REVENGE OF RAIN-IN-THE-FACE

In that desolate land and lone,
Where the Big Horn and Yellowstone
Roar down their mountain path,
By their fires the Sioux chiefs
Muttered their woes and griefs,
And the menace of their wrath.

"Revenge!" cried Rain-in-the-Face,
"Revenge upon all the race
Of the White Chief with yellow hair!"
And the mountains dark and high
From their crags re-echoed the cry
Of his anger and despair.

In the meadow, spreading wide
By woodland and river-side,
The Indian village stood;
All was silent as a dream,
Save the rushing of the stream
And the blue-jay in the wood.

In his war-paint and his beads,
Like a bison among the reeds,
In ambush the Sitting Bull

Lay, with three thousand braves,
Crouched in the clefts and caves,
Savage, unmerciful.

Into the fatal snare
The White Chief with yellow hair,
And his three hundred men,
Dashed headlong, sword in hand!
But of that gallant band
Not one returned again.

The sudden darkness of death
Overwhelmed them, like the breath
And smoke of a furnace fire;
By the river's bank, and between
The rocks of the ravine,
They lay in their bloody attire.

But the foeman fled in the night,
And Rain-in-the-Face, in his flight,
Uplifted high in air
As a ghastly trophy, bore
The brave heart that beat no more,
Of the White Chief with yellow hair.

Whose was the right and the wrong?
Sing it, oh funeral song,
With a voice that is full of tears,
And say that our broken faith
Wrought all this ruin and scath.
In the Year of a Hundred Years.

—H. W. LONGFELLOW

Why The Failure?

It has often been asked, if Custer's defeat was not due to Major Reno's failure to push the fight. That is a question about which there is much difference of opinion even among those who were engaged, and it is one that to my mind, is impossible to answer with any degree of certainty.

The ability to anticipate any and every contingency that might arise in a battle with a foe of unknown strength and position, is seldom given to mankind. Viewing the matter from afar, and from a military standpoint, with the successful accomplishment of General Custer's plan solely in mind, it is not difficult for some to think that Reno should have stayed in the fight where he began it, regardless of the cost. That Major Reno was not in a proper condition to handle the desperate situation in which he found himself is proved by his own words, as well as the personal observations and statements of several men who were under his command; of this however General Custer was not aware, and neither the officers nor men under Reno felt like saying much about the matter.

In an editorial of the Northwestern Christian Advocate of September 7th 1904, under the title Why General Custer Perished, occurs the following deeply significant statement, "—Major Reno himself told the late Reverend Dr. Arthur Edwards, the editor of the Northwestern, and Reno's faithful friend, 'that his strange actions at the battle of the Little Bighorn, were due to the fact that he was drunk.' "[1]

1. Ed. note: While it has been acknowledged that alcohol was carried by some on the campaign, the charge that Reno was intoxicated during the engagement is not supported by the testimony at the Reno court of inquiry. See Robert M. Utley, ed., *The Reno Court of Inquiry*, pp. 372–81.

Whiskey

[A titled page contained in W.O. Taylor's notes, taken from *The Arikara Narrative*, page 206.]

"James Coleman and John Smith went up the river on the Far West and met the expedition on the Powder River. . . . At that point Coleman was put off for a few days to sell liquor. Canteens, holding three pints were sold for $1.00 a pint. The liquor was brought in 45 gallon barrels and the finer brands (for officers?) were in bottles and packed in casks. When the army moved, the traders followed, going on the boat to the mouth of the Rosebud, where they again sold liquor. Then they went back to the mouth of the Tongue River where Miles City is now and Coleman has lived since. According to Coleman's report the expedition netted them forty thousand dollars from June to December, 1876." [1]

At the Court of Inquiry held at Chicago November 25th, 1879, Major Reno admitted that he had liquor in his possession at 9 o'clock p.m. on June 25th, but no questions were asked in reference to a time earlier than this. [2] Therefore, under all the circumstances, I have personally no doubt whatever that if Major Reno had maintained his position, either mounted or dismounted, for but a few moments longer, his entire command would have suffered the same fate that befell Custer. For what General Custer, quick witted, clear headed and resourceful could not do with five Companies, it is hard to believe that Reno could do with three, even if that latter had the advantage of a good position. [3]

1. Ed. note: For years after the battle, Indian participants, when interviewed regarding their memories of the fight, spoke of recovering canteens from the field that contained copious amounts of liquor. The youth and inexperience of many of Custer's troops may have led them to rely on liquid courage during the battle. This may have contributed to the disorganization on the retreat up Custer Ridge.
2. Ed. note: See *The Reno Court of Inquiry*, p. 413.
3. Ed. note: This analysis was overwhelmingly supported by the majority of the witnesses who testified at the court of inquiry. See *The Reno Court of Inquiry*, pp. 220, 261, 263, 323, and 326.

This conclusion is due to my own knowledge of the very much demoralized condition of our commander, the close proximity to the Indian village of our little force of three small troops, whose position, if we had remained there, would have been unknown to either General Custer or to Captain Benteen, both of whom were several miles away and on the opposite side of a river which was bordered by high and almost impossible bluffs.

That Major Reno should have hesitated to seek out General Custer immediately after his disastrous retreat is not to be wondered at. What acceptable excuse could he offer after such a brief fight in the bottom? No Commander, and General least of all, would be inclined to accept any excuse, for what would have seemed to him, to put it very mildly, as but a half hearted attempt to obey his orders.

Leaving Major Reno's actions out of the case, I feel that over-confidence in himself [Custer], his officers and regiment, together with his underestimating the number of the Indians until it was too late to change his plan of battle, were the two principal causes of his defeat. Had he accepted the offer of the four Troops of the Second Cavalry made him by General Terry, his plan of battle would have undoubtedly been different, and the result likewise.

General Custer

No better description can be given General Custer, as he appeared to one of the rank and file who for nearly five years followed him up and down our western frontier, than to use the language of one of his Regimental officers, who was not only a loyal friend, but a keen student of human nature and a great lover of the truth. This officer says in part: "He was a born soldier, and specifically a born Cavalryman. Remarkable for his keenness and accuracy in observation, he was never more in his element than when mounted on 'Dandy', his favorite horse and riding at the head of his Regiment. He once said to me, 'I would rather be a private in the Cavalry, than a line officer in the Infantry.' He was the personification of bravery and dash, his most bitter enemies never accused him of cowardice. If he had only added discretion to his valor he would have been a perfect soldier. . . . He was impatient of control, and liked to act independently of others and take all the risk and all the glory to himself: . . . . . . A man of great energy and remarkable endurance, he could out ride almost any man in his regiment, and was sometimes too severe in forcing marches, but he never seemed to get tired himself, and he never expected his men to be so.

A stone lithograph of General Custer autographed to W. O. Taylor from Custer's widow, Elizabeth.

In cutting our way through the Black Hills I have often seen him take an axe and work as hard as any of the pioneers, . . . With all his bravery and self-reliance, his love of independent action, Custer was more dependent than most on the kind approval of his fellows, he was vain and ambitious, and fond of display, but he had none of those great vices which are so common in the army. He never touched liquor in any form and did not smoke, chew or gamble, . . . In temperament he was sanguine and ardent, he was sometimes abrupt in manner, but kind of heart. In his circle he was fond of fun, genial and pleasant in manner, a loving and devoted husband. . . . and his loss will be felt by those who won a place in his affection."[1]

In 1913, the Superintendent of the Custer Battlefield National Cemetery sent to the writer a little sagebrush from the Custer Battlefield.

1. This description of Custer is from Cyrus T. Brady, *Indian Fights and Fighters*.

To a Sage bush from the Custer Battlefield

Oh bush of sage from Custer's field,
What memories you adorn
Of those sad days, long years ago,
Upon the Little Horn

The long hard ride up the Divide,
The rush down to the valley
The river crossed, the reckless charge,
Repulse, the rout and rally

From clouds of dust defiant yells,
And bullets vicious singing
With faces set and steady rein,
We sent our cheers a ringing

They all come back, those anxious hours,
Spent on the barren hill
The scattered dead with staring eyes,
Are in my memory still

Now planted in an alien soil,
The hope is you may thrive
Though memories sad of by gone days,
Are by you kept alive

—William O. Taylor

Unknown Remains, Custer Battle, June 25, 1876.   From Photo Taken One Year Later.

Herbert A. Coffeen, Publisher, Sheridan, Wyo.

Custer Battlefield

July 2nd 1877, an expedition under the command of Colonel Michael V. Sheridan, consisting of Troop I Seventh Cavalry, Lieutenant Nowlan commanding, with Lieutenant Hugh L. Scott as second officer, and accompanied by George Herendeen and C.J. Berendotte, both of whom had been in Reno's command, a photographer, and several civilian friends of Colonel Sheridan, arrived at the battlefield for the purpose of recovering the remains of the officers who fell in battle on the 25th of June, 1876. The party remained in camp on the site of the Indian village for several days. The time was spent in recovering the scattered remains of the enlisted men and gathering the bodies of the officers for reburial in the East. They had with them ten rough boxes, in which were placed what was supposed to be the remains of General Custer, Captains Custer, Yates, and Keogh. Lieutenants Calhoun, Cooke, Smith, McIntosh, Hodgson, and Reily. So far as known the remains were distributed as follows: General Custer at West Point, New York; Captain Keogh at Auburn, New York; Lieutenant W.W. Cooke, at Hamilton, Canada; Lieutenant Hodgson at Philadelphia, Pennsylvania. Lieutenant Reily's resting place is not known to me.[1] Captains Custer and Yates, with Lieutenants Smith, Calhoun, and McIntosh, were buried at Fort Leavenworth, Kansas. Lieutenant Crittenden's body was buried where he fell, at his father's request.

"The war whoop sounds no more with blast of bugles, Where, straight into a slaughter pen with his three hundred men, rode the chief with the Yellow hair."
— John Greenleaf Whittier

Opposite: Unknown remains, battle of the Little Bighorn, from a photo taken one year later.

---

1. Ed. note: Van Reily was interred at Washington, D.C.

The bodies of Dr. Lord, Lieutenants Harrington, Sturgis, and Porter were never found to be recognized, and they doubtless rest with the bones of the enlisted men, in the trench at the base of the monument.

The Custer Battlefield, lying within the limits of the Crow Indian Reservation, was announced a National Cemetery August 1, 1879. In July, 1881, a granite block, simple in form, but massive and heavy, was erected by the government on the summit of the ridge, near where Custer fell. On it was inscribed the names of all who fell on that field and Reno's engagement. A trench was dug ten feet from the base of the monument and on the four sides, and in it was placed all the remains that could be found, which were not removed as before stated. A small marble marker, with the inscription "U.S. Soldier, 7th Cavalry, fell here, June 25th, 1876" marks the spot where each enlisted man's body was found. The markers for the officers being the same with the exception of the inscription. Down toward the river, on a little plateau, is a section devoted to the remains of U.S. soldiers who were killed at Fort Phil Kearny, and to other soldiers from the many abandoned fort cemeteries in the northwest.

In 1909 there had been 1402 burials in this Cemetery, among them being six members of the Seventh Cavalry who died at Fort Lincoln, North Dakota. Five of the six died between July and December 31, 1876. Among the five were two enlisted men who had received serious wounds in the Battle of the Little Bighorn, June 25th, 1876. These two men were David Cooney, of I Troop, who died July 21, 1876, and Frank Braun, of M Troop, who died October 4, 1876. It seems a little singular that the bodies of these two men, after lying in a little fort cemetery for many years, should be taken back hundreds of miles and reburied within a very short distance of the spot where they had received their death-causing wound.

* * *

"In July, 1881, a granite block, simple in form, but massive and heavy, was erected by the government on the summit of the ridge near where Custer fell. On it was inscribed the names of all who fell on that field and Reno's engagement."

Monument Custer Battlefield.

WITH CUSTER ON THE LITTLE BIGHORN

This battlefield is one of great interest to many people owing to the prominence of General Custer and the peculiar circumstances under which the battle was fought to its disastrous result. General Sherman, then head of the Army, visited it in 1877, as did General Phil Sheridan and the visitors since then are to be numbered among the thousands. So strong is the attraction to some that they have made repeated visits, and the photographer as well as the relic hunter was ever present.

The Superintendent of the cemetery wrote me, in 1909, that, "he had set 25 new headstones on the battlefield this summer, to replace those that had been defaced by relic hunters," and had "also removed the wooden cross marking the spot where Custer fell, replacing it with a marble headstone." The marble marker on the spot where Captain Tom Custer fell, seems, from a photograph, to have suffered the most, this may have been due to his connection with the arrest of Rain-in-the-Face, who so terribly mutilated the General's brother.

Reno's battlefield on the bluff, has been reserved by the government, and "no change is noticeable", writes one of my former comrades who had visited it.[2] "The rifle pits are still to be seen, and the bleached bones of the horses and mules as well", but down in the bottom where the attack first began there had been quite a change since that June day in 76.

"A railroad now comes down the valley, following for a distance the line of Reno's charge, and where he dismounted his troops to fight on foot is a 'Siding' and near it a little flag station bearing the well remembered name of *Gary Owen*.[3] The grove of large cottonwood trees into which we took our horses for shelter, and which came near being a deathtrap for all of us, had been cut away, the largest trees being floated down the river and sawed up into building material for the construction of Fort Custer. The land is a part of the Crow Reservation and where Reno made his attack, and retreat, had been allotted to, and is now, 1909, owned by the following Crow Indians; Spotted Buffalo, Bull-Goes-Hunting, Pretty Enemy, and Kills-One-With Rope."

2. In 1909.
3. Ed. note: "Gary Owen" is Gaelic for Owen's Garden, a working-class suburb of Limerick, Ireland. The words of this Irish drinking song, which was written around 1775, were inspired by a series of events that took place in Owen's Garden during that time. When an economic depression forced many individuals into debtor's court, such harsh and unfair penalties were imposed on them that the local men revolted, refusing to submit to the court's injustice. The jaunty tune, a favorite of General Custer's, was chosen as the Seventh Cavalry's regimental fight song, and it continues in that role today. (See Ernest L. Reedstrom, *Bugles, Banners & War Bonnets*, p. 190.)

Little-Big-Horn River.

Coming over the old trail from the Rosebud and reaching the
top of the Divide we come in sight of the Little-Big-Horn wind-
-ing its way in a Northwesterly direction to its junction with the
main stream. South are the bold cliffs and dark canyons of
the mountains, over twenty miles away. North, tumbling
and rolling toward the Yellowstone in alternate intervals
and ridge, the treeless upland prairie stretches to the horizon
westward the eye roams over what seems to be a broad flat
valley beyond the stream, but the stream itself, called by the
Sioux "the Greasy Grass," is hidden from sight under the steep
bluffs that hem it in on the East.

Rising in the foot hills of the Big Horn Mountains of the north-
-ern end, it drains a low valley between the Wolf mountains
and the Big Horn river. some of the mountains of the Big Horn
range are perpetually covered with snow and the waters of
this little river is the clearest and coldest of any that we
had met. in width the river at this point was about sixty
feet, and its average depth some three feet, the general course
was northwesterly but for short, abrupt turns, it exceeded
any stream I ever saw. The timber, of which there was
considerble, consisted of large Cottonwood, Boxelder and some
Ash, the underbrush, of willows Roses, Dogwood, Bullberrys,
Cherry and Black Currant, the meadows were profusely covered

The Little Bighorn River

Coming over the old trail from the Rosebud and reaching the top of the divide we come in sight of the Little Bighorn winding its way in a northwesterly direction to its junction with the main stream. South are the bald cliffs and dark canyons of the mountains over twenty miles away. North, tumbling and rolling toward the Yellowstone in alternate interval and ridge, the treeless upland prairie stretched to the horizon. Westward the eye roams over what seems to be a broad flat valley beyond the stream, but the stream bed itself, called by the Sioux "the Greasy Grass", is hidden from sight under the steep bluffs that hem it in on the east.

Rising in the foothills of the Bighorn Mountains of the northern end, it drains a low valley between the Wolf mountains and the Bighorn river. Some of the mountains of the Bighorn range are perpetually covered with snow and the water of this little river is the clearest and the coldest of any that we had met. In width, the river at this point was about sixty feet, and its average depth some three feet, the general course was northwesterly but for short, abrupt turns, it exceeded any stream I ever saw. The timber, of which there was considerable, consisted of large cottonwood, box elder and some ash; the underbrush, of willows, roses, dogwood, mulberries, cherry and black currant. The meadows were profusely covered with many well known wild flowers; wild rye, barley, and oat grass seemed to flourish there and it is easy to see why it was considered by the Indians as a most desirable summer camp. General Sheridan, with a party, passed over this ground in July, 1877, and in his report it says, "The valley at this season was a continuous meadow, with grass nearly high enough to tie the tops from each side across a horses back. This was the country of the buffalo and hostile Sioux only last year. There are no signs of either now, but in their place we found prospectors, immigrants and tramps."

Soldier Couriers who Courted Death

July 9th, 1876, in answer to a call from General Terry for volunteers to carry dispatches to General Crook, three soldiers of Captain Clifford's Company, [E. 7th Inf.] James Bell, William Evans, and Benjamin H. Stewart, offered to make the attempt, although it was known that their route lay in the same direction, and close vicinity to where the victorious Sioux were headed. The country was swarming with Indians, and the prospect of these three men successfully passing through the Indian lines and finding General Crook's command, was certainly a most dubious one, but they were willing to try.

Late in the afternoon Lieutenant Roe, with his troops of the Second Cavalry and accompanied by the three daring men, crossed the Yellowstone at Fort Pease and proceeded some twelve miles up Tullock's Fork. Here they halted and when it grew dark, about 8:15 p.m., the three men started on their dangerous journey. The Cavalry returned to our camp on the Yellowstone where they arrived about ten o'clock, their object, to mask the departure of the scouts from the watchful eyes of the Indians hovering around our camp, being accomplished.

The route taken by the three Couriers must have carried them close to, if not right over the Custer battlefield. They traveled by night only and lay in some secluded spot during the day, taking turns in sleeping and watching. While en route they crossed a large Indian trail and several small ones, arrived at General Crook's camp on Goose Creek about eight miles north of old Fort Phil Kearny, "on the 12th of July," says Bourke in his book *On the Border with Crook*, who adds; "Three men, dirty, ragged, dressed in the tatters of army uniforms, rode into camp,—in the dress of each was sewed a copy of the one message which revealed the terrible catastrophe happening to the Companies under General Custer. These three modest heroes had ridden across the country in the face of unknown dangers, and had performed the duty confined to them in a manner that challenged the admiration of every man in our camp. I have looked in vain through the leaves of the Army register to see their names inscribed on the roll of commissioned officers and I feel sure that ours is the only army in the world in which such conspicuous courage, skill and efficiency would have gone absolutely unrecognized." The soldiers on their return reached our camp July 25.

It seems that General Terry, realizing the risk his soldier couriers had taken, took the precaution a few days after their departure to send a party of four Crow Indians to Crook so that the latter might surely understand the exact situation in the north. The four Crows reached Crook on the 19th of July. Two of the soldiers had a previous experience as dispatch carriers for on the 27th of May, Bell and Stewart had volunteered to carry dispatches from General Gibbon, to General Terry who was down the Yellowstone in a small skiff, and met General Terry near the Powder river and returned with him June 9th on the steamer *Far West*. Of the subsequent history of these three soldier couriers I have learned but little. Daniel Dommitt, a former member of their Company informed me in a letter, dated November 18, 1913, that "Stewart left the service early in 1877; Bell retired a Corporal of the 7th Infantry about 1897 and died at Fort Logan, Colorado shortly afterwards. Evans also left the service and died some years ago at Greely Colorado. Both of them, Evans and Bell, were appointed messengers at department headquarters, St. Paul, and Chicago, Illinois, but Evans, who was somewhat wild, did not hold his position but a few years."

The Regular Fighting Man

As many people have never seen a United States Cavalryman in his campaign dress, I am tempted to describe my own costume when engaged in the battle of the Little Bighorn, a costume which varied little if any from the rest of my comrades.

A pair of pants that had once been blue, and made of as good a grade of shoddy as the patriotic contractor could afford, had become, through the hard usage given them by months of active service and several patches made from a grain-bag, rather dilapidated as well as dirty, used as they were to sleep in as well as ride in. An old black campaign hat, contracted for during the Rebellion, with a very wide brim that had hooks and eyes on it, front and rear so that it might be made to appear in shape at least like the chapeau of a Major General, but the handling that it got and the rain and wind gave it an appearance unlike anything I ever saw on the head of a man.[1] Some of the Companies like L, F, and C, refused to wear them and purchased out of their private funds, a hat of much better shape and quality. Owing to the cheap material and its great width the brim of my hat had become separated from the crown for nearly one half the way round, and in consequence I was sometimes looking over the brim and sometimes, under it. A cheap, coarse, outing shirt, the color of a dusty road, and shy of buttons, was garnished by a large handkerchief that had once been white, the sleeves of the shirt rolled up to the elbow. The blouse, a thin dark blue garment, was strapped to the pommel of the saddle for the day was quite warm. A pair of short-legged boots from

1. Ed. note: Taylor is referring to the 1872 campaign hat, which was disliked by many cavalrymen as being too hot and uncomfortable for regular wear.

which the blackening had long since disappeared, and were now of a russet color, completed our uniform. Around the waist a canvas belt full of cartridges, below it another belt carrying a Colt's revolver, while from another, broad leather belt passing over the left shoulder swung a Springfield carbine. Rolled up and strapped to the saddle, was carried a blanket, piece of shelter tent and an overcoat, while in various other places on the saddle were hobbles, lariat, canteen, and haversack. The saddle pockets contained an extra horseshoe, nails, cartridges, currycomb and brush and sometimes a towel and piece of soap, as well as any little extras that a soldier might fancy. His quart cup was generally strapped to the saddle pocket. It was not always an easy

thing to get into the saddle with all its impediments, or to get out again. A cavalryman of that period, after a long campaign in an unsettled country was indeed a sight.

Rare photo of trooper Howard Weaver, Troop A, 7th Cavalry, 1876, wearing an 1872-pattern campaign hat.

Relics of the Battle

Among the trophies captured by Captain Anson Mills from the Indians at Slim Buttes, Sept 9, 1876, were a Seventh Cavalry Guidon, a gauntlet marked with Captain Keogh's name, orderly books, saddles, and several letters written by officers and soldiers to friends in the East.

* * *

At Fort Peck, Montana, General Hazen reported November 2, 1876 that, "A dozen 7th Cavalry horses were left here by the Sioux in their flight, so poor as to be barely able to winter, also a paymaster's check for $127.00, given to Captain Yates, endorsed by Lieutenant Cooke, which was taken in the Custer fight. The check was turned over to the agent and awaits a claimant."

* * *

Mrs. E.B. Custer received from General Miles in 1881, the map case carried by her husband in the battle. This case was secured from some of the hostiles who surrendered to General Miles that year.[1]

* * *

Mrs. James Calhoun had the good fortune to obtain possession of her husband's watch through the efforts of her brother-in-law Lieutenant Calhoun, who purchased it from some Indians in the Department of the Platte.

1. Ed. note: This map case was among the many Custer-related artifacts offered for sale at public auction in San Francisco in 1995.

*   *   *

The watch carried by Lieutenant Crittenden was also secured and returned to his father, under circumstances with which I am not familiar.

*   *   *

From the bands surrendering at Red Cloud and Spotted Tail Agencies many relics of the Custer tragedy were obtained. Among other things secured was a heavy gold ring, surmounted with a bloodstone seal, engraved with a Griffin, which had formerly belonged to Lieutenant Van Reily of the Seventh Cavalry who perished on that day. This interesting relic was returned to his mother in Washington D.C.

*   *   *

The Sioux War of 1876 cost for actual field expenses, $2,312,531.00; 283 men were killed and 125 wounded.

[REPORT OF THE SECRETARY OF WAR, 1886]

Relic Colt Model 1860 Army revolver, identified on the accompanying leather plaque as "found on the field of the Custer massacre 1876."

As Others See Us

"*Greed and avarice* on the part of the Whites in other words, the Almighty Dollar, is at the bottom of nine tenths of all our Indian troubles."

[GENERAL GEORGE CROOK]

* * *

"Next to the crime of slavery the foulest blot on the escutcheon of the Government of the United States is its treatment of the so called wards of the Nation."

[COLONEL RICHARD I. DODGE, U.S. ARMY]

* * *

"During the 27 years of my experience with the Indian question I have never known a band of Indians to make peace with our Government and then break it, or leave their reservations, without some ground of complaint."

[GENERAL CROOK, SEPT. 27, 1879]

* * *

General Miles in his report of the capture of Chief Joseph, says, "—they have been friends of the white race from the time their country was first explored,—they have been, in my opinion, grossly wronged in years past."

* * *

In speaking with the Campaign of 1876 and the means chosen by the whites to coerce the Indians to a surrender of their hunting grounds, the late Bishop Whipple a member of the Treaty Commission of the Centennial year, said, "I know of no instance in history where a great nation has so shamefully violated its oath."

Appendix 1

Notes for

<u>With Custer on the Little Bighorn</u>

by W. O. Taylor

7th U.S. Cavalry

The following addenda were discovered with other documents located in the Taylor Collection: Notes for: With Custer on the Little Bighorn. Call no. Zc 43 876 TA, Beinecke Library, Yale University. This file includes documents and research data Taylor had collected in preparation for this manuscript. Some of the material was edited out of the file when it duplicated information in the main text. Taylor's file contained so much obscure and interesting related information on the battle of the Little Bighorn that it was included as Appendix I.

BAD HEART
Sha-Ti-Sucha

Scout George Herendeen

George Herendeen was born in Ohio about 1845. He came to Montana soon after the Civil War and much of his life or time was spent at Bozeman and vicinity, where soon becoming familiar with the country he was often employed as a scout and frontiersman. Owing to his knowledge of that part of the country he was engaged as a scout by General Gibbon in the early Spring of 1876. When Gibbon's command met General Terry at the mouth of the Rosebud, Herendeen was loaned to General Custer for the purpose of carrying dispatches, if needed. When Custer, on the morning of June 25, divided the regiment for the purpose of attacking the Indians, Herendeen, with most all of the other scouts, black, white and Indian, in fact, all except four Crows and their interpreter, Mitch Bouyer, were sent in under Major Reno. [This has always seemed quite strange to me—W.O.T.] Herendeen was left behind in the woods when Reno retreated to the bluffs, but later on escaped with others and rejoined the command. In 1877 when Colonel Sheridan's party went up to the battlefield to recover the remains of the Officers who fell with Custer, Herendeen and Charles Berendotte went also. In later years be accompanied W.M. Camp, the greatest of all students of the Custer battlefield, to that locality where several days were spent in obtaining data. Some time in the '90's he removed from Bozeman to the Fort Belknap, Indian Reservation where he was employed in various capacities until shortly before his death which occurred at Harlem, Montana in the Autumn of 1919 or 1920. He was unmarried. Credit for much of the above is due to Mr. M.L. Wilson, Bozeman, Montana.

Herendeen's Account
[FROM THE NEW YORK HERALD, JULY 1876]

. . . In the way of additional particulars of the great Indian battle, I send you the story of a scout who was cut off from Reno's command.

> [Reporter, New York *Herald*,]
> Bismarck, D.T. July 7, 1876

*   *   *

We left the Rosebud [mouth of] on the 22nd of June at 12 o'clock; marched up the Rosebud about twelve miles and encamped for the night. On the morning of the 23rd we broke camp at five o'clock and continued up the Rosebud until nine o'clock when we struck a large lodge pole trail about ten days old and followed it along the Rosebud until toward evening, when we went into camp on the trail. On the morning of the 24th we pulled out at five o'clock and followed the trail five or six miles, when we met six Crow Indian Scouts, who had been sent out the night previous by General Custer to look for the Indian Village. They said they had found fresh pony tracks and that ten miles ahead the trail was fresher. General Custer had the Officer's call blown and they assembled around him, but I did not hear what he said to them. The scouts were again sent ahead and moved along at a fast walk. We moved at one o'clock, and while the Officers were eating their lunch, the scouts came back and reported that they had found where the village had been quite recently. They moved again, with Flankers well out to watch the trail and see that it did not divide. About four o'clock we came to the place where the village had been apparently only a few days before, and went into camp two miles below the forks of the Rosebud. The scouts were again pushed out to look for the village, and at eleven o'clock at night Custer had everything packed up and followed the scouts up the right hand fork of the Rosebud. About daylight we went into camp, made coffee, and soon after it was light. The scouts brought to Custer said they had seen the village from the top of a divide that separated the Rosebud from the Little Horn river.

We moved up the creek until near its head and concealed ourselves in a ravine. It was about three miles from the head of the creek where we then were to the top of the divide where the Indian scouts said the village could be seen. And after hiding his command General Custer, with a few orderlies, galloped forward to look at the Indian camp. In about an hour Custer returned and said he could not see the Indian village, but the scouts and a half breed guide "Mitch Bouyer" said they could distinctly see it some fifteen miles off. While General Custer was looking for the Indian village the scouts came in and reported that he had been discovered, and that news was then on its way to the village that he was coming. Another scout said two Sioux war parties had stolen up and seen the commander; and on looking in a ravine nearby, sure enough fresh pony tracks were found. Custer had "Officer's call" blown, gave his order and the command was put in fighting order. The scouts were ordered forward and the regiment moved at a walk. After going about three miles the scouts reported Indians ahead, and the command then took the trail. Our way lay down a little creek, a branch of the Little Horn, and after going some six miles, we discovered an Indian lodge ahead, and Custer bore down on it at a stiff trot. In coming to it we found ourselves in a freshly abandoned Indian camp. All the lodges were gone except the one we saw, and on entering it we found it contained a dead Indian. From this point we could see into the Little Horn Valley, and observed heavy clouds of dust rising about five miles distant. Many thought the Indians were moving away, and I think General Custer thought so, for he sent word to Colonel Reno, who was ahead with three companies of the Seventh regiment, to push on the scouts rapidly and head for the dust. Reno took a steady gallop down the creek bottom three miles where it emptied into the Little Horn, and found a natural ford across Little Horn River. He started to cross, when the scouts came back and called out to him to hold on, that the Sioux were coming in large numbers to meet him. He crossed over, however, formed his companies on the prairie in line of battle, and moved forward at a trot but soon took a gallop. The Valley was about three fourth of a mile wide, on the left a line of low, round hills, and on the right the river bottom covered with a growth of cottonwood trees and bushes. After scattering shots were fired from the hills and a few from the river bottom and Reno's skirmishers returned the shots. He advanced about a mile from the ford to a line of timber on the right and dismounted his men to fight on foot. The horses were sent into the timber, and the men forward on the prairie and advanced toward the Indians. The Indians, mounted on ponies, came across the prairie and opened a heavy fire on the soldiers. After skirmishing for a few minutes Reno fell back to his horses in the timber. The Indians moved to his left and rear, evidently with the intention of cutting him off from the ford. Reno ordered his men to mount and move through the timber, but as his men got into the saddle the Sioux, who had advanced in the timber, fired at close range and killed one soldier. Colonel Reno then commanded the men to dismount, and they did so, but he soon ordered them to mount again, and moved out on to the open prairie. The command headed for the ford, pressed closely by Indians in large numbers, and at every moment the rate of speed was increased, until it became a dead run for the ford. The Sioux, mounted on their swift ponies, dashed up by the side of the soldiers and fired at them, killing both men and horses. Little resistance was offered, and it was complete rout to the ford. I did not see the men at the ford, and do not know what took place further than a good many were killed when the command left the timber. Just as I got out, my horse stumbled and fell and I was dismounted, the horse running away after Reno's command. I saw several soldiers who were dismounted, their horses having been killed or run away. There were also some soldiers mounted who had remained behind, I should think in all as many as thirteen soldiers, and seeing no chance of getting away, I called on them to come into the timber and we would stand off the Indians. Three of the soldiers were wounded, and two of them so badly they could not use their arms. The soldiers wanted to go out, but I said no, we can't get to the ford, and besides, we have wounded men and must stand by them. The soldiers still wanted to go, but I told them I was an old frontiersman, understood Indians, and if they would do as I said I would get them out of the scrape, which was no worse than scrapes I had been in before. About half of the men were mounted, and they wanted to keep their horses with them, but I told them to let the horses go and fight on foot. We stayed in the bush about three hours, and I could hear heavy firing below in the river, apparently about two miles distant. I did not know who it was, but knew the Indians were fighting some of our men, and learned afterward it was Custer's command. Nearly all the Indians in the upper part of the valley drew off down the river, and the fight with Custer lasted about one hour, when the heavy firing ceased. When the shooting below began to die away I said to the boys "come, now is the time to get out." Most of them did not go, but waited for night. I told them the Indians would come back and we had better be off at once. Eleven of the thirteen said they would go, but two stayed behind. I deployed the men as skirmishers and we moved forward on foot toward the river. When we had got nearly to the river we met five Indians on ponies, and they fired on us. I returned the fire and the Indians broke and we then forded the river, the water being heart deep. We finally got over, wounded men and all, and headed for Reno's command, which I could see drawn up on the bluffs along the river about a mile off. We reached Reno in safety. We had not been with Reno more than fifteen minutes when I saw the Indians coming up the valley from Custer's fight. Reno was then moving his whole command down the ridge toward Custer. The Indians crossed the river below Reno and swarmed up the bluff on all sides. After skirmishing with them Reno went back to his old position which was on one of the highest fronts along the bluffs. It was now about five o'clock, and the fight lasted until it was too dark to see to shoot. As soon as it was dark Reno took the packs and saddles off the mules and horses and made breastworks of them. He also dragged the dead horses and mules on the line and sheltered the men behind them. Some of the men dug rifle pits with their butcher knives and all slept on their arms. At the peep of day the Indians opened a heavy fire and a desperate fight ensued, lasting until ten o'clock. The Indians charged our position three or four times, coming up close enough to hit our men with stones, which they threw by hand. Captain Benteen saw a large mass of Indians gathering on his front to charge, and ordered his men to charge on foot and scatter them. Benteen led the charge and was upon the Indians before they knew what they were about and killed a great many. They were evidently much surprised at this offensive movement, and I think in desperate fighting Benteen is one of the bravest men I ever saw in a fight. All the time he was going about through the bullets, encouraging the soldiers to stand up to their work and not let the Indians whip them; he went among the horses and pack mules and drove out the men who were skulking there, compelling them to go into the line and do their duty. He never sheltered his own person once during the battle, and I do not see how he escaped being killed. The desperate charging and fighting was over at about one o'clock, but firing was kept up on both sides until late in the afternoon. I forgot to state that about ten o'clock in the forenoon, and soon after Benteen made his charge, the men began to clamor for water, many of them had not tasted water for thirty-six hours and the fighting and hot run parched their throats, some had their tongues swollen and others could hardly speak. The men tried to eat hardtack, but could not raise enough saliva to moisten them, several tried grass but it stuck to their lips, and not one could spit or speak plainly. The wounded were reported dying for want of water, and a good many soldiers volunteered to go to the river to get some water or perish in the attempt. We were fighting on the bluffs about 700 yards from the river, and a ravine led down from the battlefield close to the river's edge. The men had to run over an open space of about 100 yards to get into the head of the ravine and this open space was commanded by the Indians on the bluffs. The soldiers, about fifty strong, dashed over the open plateau and entered the ravine. They rushed down it to the mouth and found it closely guarded by a party of Indians posted in the timber across the river. The water could be approached to within about thirty feet under cover, but then one had to step out on the river bank and take the Indians fire. The boys ran the gauntlet bravely, some would dash down to the river with camp kettles, fill them and then take shelter in the bend of the ravine, behind the rocks, and where canteens were filled and carried up the hill. Before all the men and wounded were supplied one man was killed and six or seven wounded in this desperate attempt. One man had the bone of his leg shattered by a ball, and it has since been amputated. About two o'clock the Indians began drawing off, but kept skirmishing until late in the afternoon, and near dark all drew off. We now got water for the animals, many of them being almost dead, and they were put out to graze on the hillside. In the evening Major Reno changed his position and fortified the new one, it being higher and stronger than the old one. We expected the Indians would renew the attack next day, but in the morning not an Indian was to be seen. Every one felt sure that Crook or Terry was coming to our relief, and Major Reno sent out runners. About ten o'clock the glad intelligence was received that General Terry with a large column of troops, was moving up the valley six miles distant, and the head of his column soon came in sight.

In reply to questions [from the *Herald* reporter] , Mr. Herendeen said: "I went in with the scouts on the left of Reno's line, there were about sixty of us, thirty-five being Ree Indians, six friendly Sioux, six Crows and the rest white men. I saw Bloody Knife, a Ree scout, throw up his arm and fall over, and I think he was killed. The two cavalry soldiers I left in the timber when I went out I have no doubt were killed, as they have not been seen since. I saw Lieutenant McIntosh soon after he fell. He had his horse shot under him early in the action, and at the time he was killed he was riding a soldier horse; he was shot on the river bank while riding back to the ford. I saw Lieutenant Hodgson also. His horse was shot and he was wounded. His horse fell into the river near the opposite bank of ford, and to help himself up the steep bank Hodgson caught hold of a horse's tail and had got up the bank when an Indian sharpshooter picked him off. Custer's packs were with the rear and the Indians did not get any of them, neither did they get any mules. Most of Custer's horses were shot in the action, and I do not believe the Indians got over one hundred animals in the fight. I think some of our men were captured alive and tortured. I know the colored scout Isaiah was, for he had small pistol balls in his legs from the knees down, and I believe they were shot into him while alive. Another man had strips of skin cut out of his body. Hordes of squaws and old gray haired Indians were roaming over the battlefield howling like mad. The squaws had stone mallets and mashed in the heads of the dead and wounded. Many were gashed with knives and some had their noses and other members cut off. The heads of four white soldiers were found in the Sioux camp that had been severed from the trunks, but the bodies could not be found on the battlefield or in the village. Our men did not kill any squaws, but the Ree Indians did. The bodies of six squaws were found in the little ravine. I think the Indian village must have contained about 6,000 people, 3,000 of whom were warriors. The Indians fought Reno first and then went to fight Custer, after which they came back to finish Reno. The same Indians were in all the attack. I think the Indians were commanded by Sitting Bull in person. There were eight or nine other chiefs in the field. I saw five chiefs and each one carried a flag for their men to rally around. Some of the flags were red, others yellow, white and blue, and one a black flag. All the chiefs handled their warriors splendidly. I think Crazy Horse and his band were in the fight. The Indians must have lost as many men in killed and wounded as the whites did. Custer's men made a good fight, and no doubt killed a great many Indians. I don't think a single man escaped from Custer's part of the field. They were completely surrounded on every side by at least 2,500 warriors."

*   *   *

A staff officer has informed me that the haste of General Custer in attacking the Indians was entirely due to himself. General Terry had informed General Custer that he [Terry] would be at the mouth of the Little Horn river on the 26th of June, and Custer might expect to find him there with Gibbon's column. Terry marched as agreed upon, but found the road much more difficult than he had anticipated. The infantry suffered terribly on the 25th for water, the march being over a high and dry divide under a boiling sun. Terry pushed on from four o'clock in the morning until four in the evening, where the infantry, completely exhausted, were left in camp, and Terry continued the march with Brisbin's cavalry all night through a rainstorm and darkness. At daylight on the morning of the 26th Terry was in sight of the mouth of the Little Horn and had kept his promise to Custer to be there early on the 26th of June. At eight o'clock Terry heard from Crow scouts of Custer's disaster, and deeply regretted his haste in attacking the Indian camp on the 25th. If Custer had struck the Little Horn one day later or deferred his attack twenty-four hours later, Terry could have cooperated with him, and, in all probability, have prevented the disaster. A Crow Indian scout named "Curley" came in the day after the battle and stated he was in the fight with Custer. He says the fight lasted over one hour, Custer contending against ten times his number. The men fought splendidly until the Big Chief [Custer] fell, and then they became somewhat demoralized. Most of the Officers and men had been killed before Custer. "Curley" says the Indians fought Custer on foot and charged his men again and again. He thought a great many more Indians were killed in the fight than there were in Custer's command.[?] "Curley" is a truthful Indian, and his statement may be relied upon.

*   *   *

Custer Massacre

[COPIED FROM "TALKS AND THOUGHTS", OF THE INDIAN STUDENTS, HAMPTON INSTITUTE, HAMPTON, VA, DECEMBER, 1888, JANUARY 1889.]

When I was a small boy I saw General Custer and his army at Yankton, (1873). When they went away my father went with them. I wish to give a brief sketch of this so called Custer Massacre, as it was told to me by a person who was engaged in it, and who is also now a good and faithful student of this school. Though it may be imperfect in some details, yet I think it a straight-forward account.

*   *   *

This is the account of it without detail; first before this massacre four tribes or bands joined the main tribe, making in all five tribes. They were wholly ignorant of the fact that they were being hunted by United States Troops. Suddenly one day about noon, while they were encamped in a long ravine, [a narrow valley] word was brought that soldiers were marching upon them. The greatest excitement and confusion followed, the women with crying babies on their backs left their tepees and retreated in a very disorderly man-ner toward a large hill about two miles distant. In the meantime all the war-riors ran for their ponies, and started off to check the advancing enemy. There was a ravine [old bed of the river] between General Custer [Major

Reno] and the Indians camping ground. Into this ravine under cover of poplar and ash trees, the young warriors awaited the enemy. In a very short time Custer [Reno] made his appearance, and when he saw the Indians were prepared for his reception, and that he could not come upon the encampment, he did a thing that was very rash and unsoldierly. Instead of falling back he immediately ordered his detachment, for his main army was some distance away, to get into line for a skirmish. To put it in the words of my friend who gave me the account in his own language, "Custer [Reno] did this thing without thinking, and anybody knew that if he presented himself as a target for an Indian he would be served as such." The skirmish began; and of course under the circumstances it could not be otherwise than one sided. There were more of the Indians, and having the advantage of concealment while the soldiers were much fewer in number, and being under great disadvantages, both in regard to number and protection and though Custer's [Reno's] men did not come near enough for the white of their eyes to be visible, yet they were in rifle range. It seemed a sin and a folly to order men to stand before such unfavorable odds. The soldiers were so rapidly shot down that at last some found that discretion was the better part of valor, and retreated without order, and the consequence was disastrous in the extreme. Men rode over each other and being frightened themselves and their horses also, the retreat was made in a very confused unmilitary order. Men running on foot and horses madly galloping, with the Indians in the rear and on their flanks was the scene caused by the blunder of a single man, and the last blunder that the men made was that instead of retreating directly from the Indians, in their excitement or perhaps through the ignorance of the extent of the Indian line, they retreated right along the line of the Indians, almost under the muzzles of their guns. This they did in order that they might get to the main army. The main army was little to the northeast of the Indians. I do not know the exact distance this main army was, but, however, not a single man of the ill fated detachment reached it, all were killed, but were not scalped as I have heard.

* * *

Word was brought soon after the destruction of the detachment that there were U.S. troops only a short distance off toward the east of the Indians encampment. The young warriors had already caught the horses whose master lay dead and also the rifles and ammunition. Some even took the uniform coats [blouses] and caps of Custer and his Five troops of dead soldiers. It was told that an Indian took General Custer's [perhaps Lieutenant McIntosh's] handsome uniform coat, cap, and sword, and when the attack on the main force was made he behaved in a military manner that would have done justice to any General that ever wore shoulder straps. It was early in the afternoon that the attack began. There were four (five) companies of the soldiers. They held their ground bravely and fought desperately, knowing that it was the only alternative and resolved to fall fighting to the last. They stood shoulder to shoulder in solid companies and the ranks were broken only by those who were shot. On the other hand the Indians were scattered over quite a range of land and some were behind rocks and kept a constant fire into the solid companies. The Companies neither made any charge or attempted to fall back. Had General Custer been alive to head his devoted followers, he no doubt would have made fierce charges upon the Indians. I was told last summer by reliable authority that Custer was noted for his fierce and reckless charges during the Civil War. The companies one after another were killed till only one company was on the field then a retreat was attempted, but it was too late. In about two hours after the attack began, there was not a living soldier to be seen.

*   *   *

This is the sad account of the fate of General Custer and his devoted followers.

*   *   *

I shall here say that it was cruel that all should be killed. And I am sure that had it not been for the reckless young men who entirely composed the Indian force, the result would have been different. Yet, again when my cheeks almost burn with shame, I think of the hard and cruel treatment that our poor ancestors were subjected to, and were driven from their land, their homes, and from the graves of their fathers and mothers without mercy, can anybody wonder then that an uncivilized and ill treated and despised nation should do what a civilized and christian nation did not do? Can this sad destruction of an aggressive army be justly called a massacre?

[NOTE: THIS ACCOUNT WAS WRITTEN BY ONE OF THE HAMPTON STUDENTS, HENRY LYMAN, A YANKTON SIOUX, WHOSE FATHER WAS AN ARMY OFFICER[1] BY THE SAME NAME WHO ALWAYS CARED FOR HIS CHILDREN AS LONG AS HE LIVED. THIS WOULD ACCOUNT FOR THE BOY'S SYMPATHY WITH THE ARMY. THE BOY MENTIONED IN THE ARTICLE, FROM WHOM HENRY LEARNED MANY OF THE DETAILS, DIED SOON AFTERWARDS. HENRY WAS GRADUATED FROM THE YALE LAW SCHOOL AND DIED ABOUT FIVE YEARS LATER.

        H.B. FRIZZELL, PRINCIPAL
        JANUARY 15, 1912]

Captain Ball's Scouting Party

Captain Ball of the 2nd cavalry with his Troop H, was sent out from Reno's field on the 28th of June and followed the trail of the departing Indians for some ten or twelve miles. He found that it led directly south toward the Bighorn Mountains. In returning to camp [where Reno's fight began] he discovered a large, fresh trail heading down the Little Bighorn toward the scene of the battle. [Colonel Gibbon's report]. Jeff Hanson in his *Conquest of the Missouri*, says on page 288, that this trail discovered by captain Ball was made by Crazy Horse's band after their fight with Crook. This does not seem to agree with Grinnell's story in "The Fighting Cheyennes", which says, page 335, "from the mouth of the Rosebud the Indians moved up that stream,

1. Probably a noncommissioned officer.—W.O.T.

then over to the head of Reno Creek—and after the men had left to fight Crook [the 17th of June] the villages moved a short distance down Reno Creek toward the Little Bighorn, and after two nights there they moved to the mouth of Reno Creek and camped there for five or six days—the day before Custer's attack the Indians moved again and camped on the great bottom of the Little Big Horn, at a place where the battle was fought."

General Custer struck an Indian trail about twenty miles up the Rosebud, which trail as we advanced became larger. And when we had reached the north fork of the Rosebud, about seventy-three miles from the Yellowstone, it turned up the north fork and over the divide toward the Little Bighorn, following down what is now called Reno Creek.

General Sheridan and the Little Bighorn 1877

General Sheridan with a part of his staff, and accompanied by General Crook, made a trip to the Bighorn country in 1877, leaving Chicago the 25th of June. On July 19th they crossed from Tongue River to the Little Bighorn river and continued down the valley of that river. In his report it is stated that "Camp 19 was pitched in a beautiful and extensive valley on the left bank of the Little Bighorn river, immediately opposite the Seventh Cavalry battle-ground of June 25th, 1876." No mention is made in this report of their visiting Custer's battlefield, but they undoubtedly did so. [W.O.T.]

"The next day fifteen miles were made, the trail ascending a high table land lying between the Big and Little Bighorn rivers, which it followed. It reached the new military post No. 2, at the junction of the Big and Little Bighorn Rivers." [this fort was, later on, named Fort Custer]— "We found post No. 2 delightfully located by Lieutenant Colonel Buell. Five steamers coming up the Bighorn were in sight, from the fort to the mouth of the Bighorn was forty-five miles by water, and thirty miles by land."

The New York Herald in its issue of June 6, 1909, contains an illustrated article by Dr. Joseph K. Dixon on the Custer battlefield, in which it is stated "At Lodge Grass, Montana, lives White-Man-Runs-Him, known in the Crow tongue as 'Miastashede-karoos'. Today despite his sixty-five years he is straight as an arrow and graceful as a pine tree, standing six feet, lithe and supple, he is the acme of quiet dignity—he has within the last year led several investigators over the very trail along which he had conducted Custer's men thirty-three years ago.— Only a few months ago, under the urgency of Dr. Joseph K. Dixon, a noted Ethnologist, who had charge of the Wanamaker expedition, the four surviving scouts, each now more than sixty years of age, trudged together to the spot where Custer fell—. Never before had those four survivors of the battle of the Little Bighorn, thus together paid their silent tribute to the dead."

Odds and Ends

Lieutenant Charles Braden of the 7th cavalry was wounded on the Yellowstone Expedition in 1873. He has written two articles for the Journal of the Cavalry Association. One in October, 1904, the other in October 1905. Colonel E.B. Fuller, Fort Leavenworth, Kansas was in 1910, the Secretary of the Association.

* * *

Camp, on the Little Missouri, oats scattered from the feed bags of Custer troops in May, 1876 germinated and attained such a growth that General Crook's men who occupied the same camping ground, on the fourth of September cut large armfuls for their horses.

* * *

Charles Corn of Thunder, Butte, South Dakota, a Sioux Indian who fought with his people against General Custer on the Little Bighorn, June 25, 1876, in reply to some question I asked him by letter, made the following statements under dates of September 15, 1909, and April 23, 1910.

"We did not know you were coming until you fired on us." There were three battles: Reno's attack, Custer's attack, and Reno besieged. [W.O.T.] "In the first fight four Indians were killed, in the second fight 21 Indians were killed, and in the third fight, up on the hill, 2 Indians were killed." "We did not know it was Custer until quite a while afterward. The second fight lasted about two hours". "One man killed himself about a mile from the other. He was riding a dark bay horse and was very fast. He shot himself through the head. He could have lived because he was riding a fast horse."

"There were five tribes of us there but the soldiers wanted to kill us so we had to fight for our lives. You tried to get our children and wives so I was willing to die fighting for them that day. I was tried that day." "To this day that battle is still fresh in my mind. I was 23 years old then so I was not afraid to face anything."

* * *

Two of the Ree scouts remained with Reno. Young Hawk and Goose, the latter was slightly wounded and was put off the steamer at Fort Buford.

* * *

Twenty-five recruits joined K Troop at St. Paul in April, 1876. General Godfrey and probably about the same number joined Troops B and G.

* * *

About one hundred horses were lost by Reno's command, being captured, killed or wounded so badly they had to be shot. [Terry's report]

* * *

John Martini, the trumpeter of M troop, rode with General Custer until ordered back with a message to his company commander, Captain Benteen. He was the last white man who saw Custer alive and lived to tell of it. In 1910 he was living at 168 Prospect Street, Brooklyn, New York. In a letter in answer to some question of mine he made the following statements. March 24, 1909. [W.O.T.] "When I left General Custer he was about 200 yards from his command. I could see the Indian village, but not Major Reno's command. I met Boston Custer while I was on my way to join Benteen. He spoke to me, it was about three miles from where I left Custer to where I met Benteen. I was about half hour, going at a gallop. Mitch Bouyer was at the head of the column when Custer gave me the message. There were also three Crows as I remember."

*   *   *

Sergeant Stanislaus Roy, 523 Park Avenue, Piqua, Ohio, in a letter to this writer dated March 11, 1909, speaks of a visit he made to the Little Bighorn battlefield in August 1909. He says—The C.B. and [?] R.R. comes down the Little Bighorn valley on the west side of the river. Not more than two hundred rode from Reno's skirmish line. The river course has changed some since and the place where our horses were led into the woods is partly a swamp now, and where we had our fighting on foot is a field fenced in and an Indian shack and a haystack right on the spot. Lieutenant McIntosh's marker is close by. Where we made the second crossing looks very natural. There is still quite a pile of horses bones on Reno's hill. The valley of the Little Bighorn is very beautiful. It is all in farms owned by the Crow Indians. The Crow Agency is three miles down the river from the monument and old Fort Custer is twelve miles below the Agency.

*   *   *

Stanislaus Roy as Corporal in A troop, was in charge of the picket guard posted on the night of June 25th. A few rode in front of the position held by

A troop. The detail consisted, besides the Corporal, of Privates Harris, Connors, Bancroft, McElurg, Gilbert, and W.O. Taylor, this writer.

* * *

Captain Robert E. Bell of the 3rd regiment, Michigan Infantry [Militia], in a very interesting letter to the writer dated at Minneapolis, Minn., May 30th, 1910, among other things states that "his uncle was in that campaign, 1876, and that with him in 1889, he followed the old trail from Fort Lincoln to the Little Bighorn." He was there again in 1910 and says the old rifle pits or trenches in which you and your commander lay on the hill tops are still there and can be easily followed, the bones of your horses are still strewn in a ragged row where the Field Hospital was located. Dr. DeWolf's marker still stands down on the point overlooking the ravine and the river. The grave of Lieutenant McIntosh across the river is surrounded by a little fence.

* * *

June 20, 1876, six Crow scouts were detailed from General Gibbon's command on the Yellowstone at the mouth of the Rosebud to serve with General Custer. With them was sent their interpreter Mitch Bouyer, a half breed. The latter was killed with Custer.

* * *

Sitting Bull. In an interview with Father Geniss, Sitting Bull said among other things, that "The soldiers, (Custer's men) who were killed were horsemen but they had no chance to fight or run away, they were surrounded too closely by our many warriors. *As they stood there waiting to be killed they were seen to look far away to the hills in all directions and we knew they were looking for the hidden soldiers in the hollow of the hills to come and help them.*" Doane Robinson says there were 63 indians killed at the Little Bighorn, June 25th, 1875. General Godfrey in 1916, June 24th, camped at the Indian School, about one mile above our bivouac of June 24th, 1876. He says our track went up Davis

Creek which has always been my belief. Reno's report of killed mentions Bloody Knife, [Ree] Bob-Tail-Bull and Utah.

W.O.T.

*   *   *

Captain Thomas M. French, Troop M 7th Cavalry was court martialed at Fort Lincoln, Dakota in 1879 and sentenced to be dismissed from the service; this was amended to suspension from rank on *half pay for one year*. Lieutenant James Sturgis was detailed to keep an itinerary of Major Reno's scouting party June 10th, but unfortunately he had his notebook with him at the time he was killed.

*   *   *

Sergeant Wm. G. Cayes and Private Ferdinand Widdemeyer of M Troop 7th Cavalry were left at Powder River with the company teams and probably one or two other Privates or Company teamsters. There were twelve pack mules to each troop. "Eighty-four men constituted a full company of cavalry in 1876, but it was seldom that a troop was full"

[JOHN RYAN]

*   *   *

From Fort Lincoln to the mouth of Powder River as we marched, was 318½ miles. [Report of Lieutenant Edward McGuire, Engineer Officer] From the mouth of the Powder River, to the mouth of the Rosebud, in an air line on the map, is 70 miles. Our route, as we marched must have been somewhat longer, maybe ten miles, making it about 80 miles. From the mouth of the Rosebud, to where Reno attacked on the Little Bighorn was, according to the record of Lieutenant George D. Wallace, about 102 miles, a total of just about 500 miles in a direct line. It was about 340 miles from Fort Lincoln to the Little Bighorn. From Reno's hill to the mouth of the Powder River was about 185 miles.

[GENERAL GODFREY]

Indian Scouts with General Miles in 1879

FROM *WAR PATH AND BIVOUAC* BY J.F. FINERTY

Little Wolf, the Cheyenne chief was regarded with respect by all the officers on account of his honesty and fearlessness. He and Brave Wolf were accounted the two best Indians in the command.[1] ". . . the Cheyennes are as proud as Lucifer, and really big. They fight like lions, . . . some of them are amazingly intelligent, and, strange as it may seem to my readers, are of gentlemanly deportment. Brave Wolf was as graceful as a courtier, and had a face of remarkable refinement.[2]

". . . people who imagine that the Aborigines possess none of the finer feelings of humanity, will, perhaps, be enlightened by the following list of remittances sent to their families by our allied Sioux and Cheyenne warriors, who had, three years before, taken part in the battle of the Little Bighorn. Their names and the amount of their pay they remitted to their families are as follows: Spotted Bear $20, White Horse $20, Spotted Wolf $20, Brown Wolf $15, Two Moons Junior $15, Henry $10, Tall Bull $10, Yellow Dog $10, Little Bull $10, Poor Elk $10, Bobtail Horse $10, Paint $10, Bull Head $10, Spotted Wolf $10, Little Horse $10 Two Moons Senior $10."

The Bad Lands of North Dakota

"Up to 1880 the country through which the Little Missouri flows remained as wild and almost as unknown as it was when the old explorers and fur traders crossed it in the early part of the century. . . . indeed, the trail made by Custer's wagon train is today one of the well known landmarks, for the deep ruts made by the wheels of the heavy wagons are in many places still as distinctly to be seen as ever."

(RANCH LIFE, BY T. ROOSEVELT, P. 101.)

1. P. 263.
2. P. 261.

Indian Village on the Little Bighorn, June 1876

Charles A. Eastman, a full blooded Sioux, educated in the eastern schools and colleges, a government official for several years at Standing Rock Agency, and who had an uncle and several cousins in the battle, places the order of the camps and number of tepees as follows: [His estimate is disputed and rightly so, I think.—W.O.T.]

> Hunkpapas, (those who dwell by themselves) 224 tepees, Gall, Crow King, Black Moon, Sitting Bull
> Sans Arcs, (without Bows) 85 tepees, Spotted Eagle, Elk Head
> Santees and Yanktonair, a remnant of the unsoldiered Hostiles of the Wimmento outback, 15 tepees, Inkpoduto[1] Brules, (Burnt Thighs) 140 tepees, Low-Dog, Little-Hawk
> Minneconjou, 190 tepees, Hump, Lame Deer, Fast Bull, Iron Starr
> Ogalalas (Wanders in the Mountains) 240 tepees, Crazy Horse, Big Road, No-Water
> Cheyenne 55 tepees, Two Moons, White Bull, Little Horse

* * *

Mr. Eastman's estimate of tepees 949, of warriors 1411.

During the winter preceding, the different bands had been located as follows:

Cheyennes on Powder River, Crazy Horse not far away,

Sitting Bull and the Tamaches on the Little Missouri. The Ellinne Canyon and Brules on the Yellowstone near the mouth of Tongue River.

* * *

Some of the lesser Chiefs and Head men were Red Dog, Kill-Eagle, Lone Wolf, Little Big Man a half breed, which Genniss is said to have been with them.

* * *

---

1. They had lately come down from Canada.

Reno's Fight, Run by Roman Rutten

TROOP M, 7TH CAVALRY

A letter from Roman Rutten, a soldier of M Troop 7th Cavalry who was in the Battle of the Little Bighorn, dated Leavenworth, Kansas, April 9, 1911 says . . . "Bloody Knife, Isaiah and Charley Reynolds were killed right out of the woods 50 feet apart. I saw Isaiah, (Dorman) he was standing and firing into the Indians. His horse was killed. As I went by him he shouted 'goodbye Rutten'. Bloody Knife and Charley Reynolds were on their horses fighting. Lorentz was shot in the woods. Scullen and Klotzblucher were killed on the flat. Stringer stood against a tree when I passed him in the woods. I don't know if he was dead or not, but that was the last known of him. I saw Corporal Hagerman of G troop as his horse was shot under him. I passed through a bunch of Indians that had him surrounded and I shouted to him to 'hold on to my horse', he was not wounded then. I afterward found his body.

"I stayed in M Troop up to 1890 (about 15 years) when I left in 1890 there was still in M troop, 1st Sergeant Ryder, Griffin, (?) Myers and Jack Donahue. Captain French died at Leavenworth. His sister had his body removed to the East. Captain Yates, Tom Custer, Lieutenant Smith, and McIntosh were also buried here, but the wife of Lieutenant McIntosh had his remains removed to Arlington early in 1910."

ROMAN RUTTEN, 720 BROADWAY, LEAVENWORTH, KANSAS.

* * *

Sergeant John Ryan continues: "of M Troop, Sergeant O'Hara and Corporal Stringer were killed in the woods as also Private Lorentz. Private Henry Gordon and Wm. Myers were killed on their way up the bluffs. Tanner and Voight were killed on the hill and were buried in one grave down in the depression where the pack mules and horses were. Frank Brown was wounded on the hill, but did not die until he reached Fort Lincoln. Corporal Scullin, and Private Klotzbucker were killed on the flat. All except Tanner and Voight were buried where they fell. Corporal McGlass carried the

Guidon which is believed was lost in crossing the river. Sergeant White and Carey were left behind but came up afterward. M Troop took about 45 men into the fight, 14 were killed and 10 wounded.

"Charley Reynolds was killed in the woods and Isaiah Dorman the colored interpreter was killed not far from him, as was also Bloody Knife. The Ree Scout, Dr. DeWolf crossed the river, but was killed on the bluffs before reaching the top. Lieutenant McIntosh was killed on the retreat to the river a short distance from the woods. It was said 'he was trying to rally his men'. A marker was put up where he fell and a little fence around it."

*   *   *

From the ford where we first crossed the river to where we dismounted to "fight on foot", was about $2^{1}/2$ miles. Reno's report says "he did not see Benteen again until about 2:30. At 12:30 [noon] he was 2 miles from the ford, rode fast, crossed the river and drove the Indians for $2^{1}/2$ miles. Our rate of speed must have been at least eight miles an hour, and we certainly could not have been fighting dismounted for over $^{1}/2$ hour." Sergeant John Ryan says "about twenty minutes". Fifteen minutes was ample time for us to reach the river, and the bluff, no one was disposed to linger on the way. Hence we should have, and undoubtedly were on the hill at, or very close to 2 o'clock. The Cheyennes say that Reno had been defeated and was on the hill before Custer drew near the river. And they also state that only ten Indians were at the ford, (north end) to open any charge that might have been made.

*   *   *

When Dull Knife Village was captured by General Miller, March 26, 1876, many articles were found that formerly belonged to the 7th Cavalry. One of the most interesting was a roster book of a first sergeant of the 7th Cavalry. The book had been captured by an Indian who had filled it with his drawings. After passing through the hands of Colonel Homer W. Wheeler and several others, Mr. George B. Grinnell secured it to take out to the Cheyennes and see if the artist who had illustrated it could be identified, and there he found that the Indian's name was High Bear. The book proved to have belonged to G Troop.

[FROM G. B. GRINNELL, THE FIGHTING CHEYENNES]

*　*　*

Sergeant Crisswell was of B Troop, so says W.D. Nugent of it, 1921. Private Holmstead of A Troop was one of the men left in the bottom and came up afterwards.

(W.D. NUGENT)

Number of Indians on the Little Bighorn
JUNE 25–26, 1876

As for the strength of the Indians attacked by General Custer, Young Two Moon, who took a part, told Mr. G.B. Grinnell that there were 200 lodges in the Cheyenne camp and there were six villages of Sioux, each one larger than the Cheyenne. Even if the Sioux villages were no larger than the Cheyenne this would make ? lodges. And besides the people occupying the lodges there were a multitude of stronger Indians from different reservations whose number cannot be estimated. Many were camped under shelter outside of the lodges. Cheyennes have told me that they believed there were more than 1500 lodges, and perhaps three or four fighting men to a lodge, a total therefore of from 4500 to 6000 men.

[FROM G. B. GRINNELL, THE FIGHTING CHEYENNES]

*　*　*

In a letter to Major D.W. Benham at Fort Ellis [?] dated "Camps on the Little Bighorn, June 28th, 1876", General Gibbon, commanding the Montana column says ". . . , roughly stated the loss of Custer's is about one half 250 men. The Indians were in great strength and were estimated to from 1200 to 2500 warriors".

Strength of the Indians

Frank Girard, a native of the Sandwich Islands, was General Crook's chief scout in 1876. He had been for several years a prisoner of the Sioux Indians and a member for some time of Crazy Horse's household. He stated that "While history says the number of Indians opposed to Custer had been given as 3000, the Sioux say that they had more than 8000."

*   *   *

A correspondent of the New York Herald [probably of Gibbon's command, or else one of the Officers—W.O.T.] under date of June 28, 1876 says, "there were estimated to have been 4000 warriors judging from the number of tepee fires. Engineer's statement."

*   *   *

General Terry, in a telegram to General Sheridan, March 24, 1876, says "the most trustworthy scout on Missouri River recently in hostile camp reports not less than 2000 lodges and that the Indians are loaded down with ammunition." And in another dispatch, May 14, three days before starting he says "it is represented that they have 1500 lodges, are confident and intend making a stand."

*   *   *

George Herendeen, a Montana scout from Gibbon's command, was with Major Reno; he says "I think the Indian village must have contained about 6000 people, 3000 of whom were warriors.

(NEW YORK HERALD, JULY 1876)

* * *

General Sheridan, in a dispatch to General Terry, dated June 6, 1876, says "Yellow Robe served at Red Cloud Agency, June 5th, six days from the hostile camp, and reports 1800 lodges were on the Rosebud—that they will fight and have about 3000 warriors."

* * *

Mitch Bouyer, one of Gibbon's scouts and interpreters loaned to Custer with whom he stayed, and fell, was heard by Lieutenant Hare, on duty with the scouts, to tell the General the morning of the fight that "it was the largest village ever collected in the Northwest." and Bouyer had been with the Indians over 30 years.

From My Friend the Indian
How Long Custer's Fight Lasted [1]

. . . Gall, Crow King, Crow Bear, Captain W.O. Wech and Kill Eagle, all of whom were in position to see the entire field covered by Custer's force and who have corroborated each other unboastingly—have told me that from the time of the first attack until the last man of Custer's command died on the battlefield, not more time elapsed than would be necessary to walk from that spot (the Agency Office, at Standing Rock) to Antelope Creek, a mile distant. It might have been a half hour altogether. Within that period all defense possible was made, including the movement from the bottom to the height, which was much less than a mile.

---

1. John A. Cockerill, in E. Hubbard, *The Teepee Book*, says one Indian told Scout Campbell that "the fight, (Custer's) lasted as long as it would take a hungry Indian to eat his dinner." And another one said that "it lasted as long as a candle would burn about one quarter of an inch." From this it is inferred that the struggle lasted about twenty-five minutes.

From My Friend the Indian

Custer's course. . . . Described by the Indians to James McLaughlin, see page 82.[1]

*   *   *

Page 130 . . . . . for more than an hour they had seen Custer's column marching along the ridge, ... page 138 . . . . . soon after detaching Reno's battalion, Custer reached the eastern end of the long, high ridge which was in full view of the Indians for a distance of quite six miles. . . . . page 146 Custer probably took the ridge as a means of announcing his coming and to divert attention from the attack of Reno. . . . . . Page 148. While his column was still silhouetted against the skyline of the ridge, Crazy Horse with the Cheyennes crossed the river and made their way into the ravine to the north and west of the ridge upon which Custer was advancing . . . Custer swung his troops to the left from the ridge, and turned down toward the river. As the men advanced into the bottom . . . . they did not falter and they were well down to the stream before the Sioux showed themselves on that shore. . . . With the first shot that was fired the truth undoubtedly dawned upon Custer that he had met a formidable foe. The Indians in considerable numbers rose up in front of them and went directly to the attack, the soldiers retreated instantly, the ridge behind and to the right of the troops . . . . they had left to go into the bottom which might afford the men a chance to defend themselves, ... While a considerable body of Indians followed and harassed the men in this movement, another and even larger body was sent around the ravine to the rear of the position arrived at by Custer . . . . . and when the Cavalry had attained that position the elevation was surrounded to the north and west, while a considerable more of the Sioux were advancing on what might be called the front of Custer's position. See page 80 . . . . pages 121–122. . . . The generalship of Gall that kept the strength of the Indians concealed from the white soldiers, in spite of the fact that the forces had been in conflict on June 17th preceding the Little Bighorn affair, when Crazy Horse actually,

---

1. All page references are to James McLaughlin, *My Friend the Indian*.

defeated General Crook.[2] *This was before the union of the hostile forces.* . . . . It was not until within an hour of the end that Custer came to know approximately the power of the enemy, ... Gall, Crow, King and Crazy Horse had plainly out generaled the commanders of the three columns sent against them (Crook, Gibbons, and Terry) in hiding their strength, and eventually choosing the spot to give battle, ... and the greater of the three war chiefs was Gall.

* * *

General Miles in June 1878, visited the Custer battlefield, and in his story "My First Fight on the Plains", says . . . . "We rode our horses at a walk over the ground from Reno's last position to the extreme right of Custer's line, where the monument is, and were 58 minutes by the watch. Had Reno's command walked half that distance, it would have been in action, moving at a smart trot or gallop as cavalry goes into action. It could have attacked the Indians in the rear easily in fifteen or twenty minutes."

* * *

Cheyenne Indians living in 1921 at Lame Deer, Montana who took part in the battle of the Little Bighorn [Mrs. A.C. (Mrs. Custer)]

Fred Ironshirt	Frank High Walking	William Wolfname
Lewis Roundstone	Bob-Tailed-Horse	Little Whiteman
Arthur Brady	Spotted Blackbird	Isaac Grasshopper
Thomas Black-Whiteman	Henry Hairy Hand	Frank Stumphorn
Zac Ridgebear	John-Bull-Thigh	Martin Bulls Keep
Wolf Chief	Badger John Issues	Little Gun

2. Battle of the Rosebud.

How Crow Indians Fight

In the Autumn of 1878, General Miles had news of an outbreak of the Bannock Indians and while passing by the old Crow Indian Reservation, tried to induce some of the Crows to accompany him, promising them food, ammunition, and all the horses they could capture from the Bannocks. The sight of his little command, some 35 men, proved at first to be an obstacle, but after he had proceeded for seven miles he was joined by small parties until there were 75 well equipped warriors. After the hostile camp had been located, a short sharp fight ensued resulting in the death of the Bannocks and the capture of the rest. While the troops were fighting the Bannocks, the Crows were rounding up the horses and soon there was not a Crow Indian or a Bannock, or a Bannock horse left in the valley. They had taken 250 horses and did not stop until they had reached their Agency 75 miles away. Some fighters those Crows.

Appendix II

Officers of the Seventh Cavalry
CAMPAIGN OF 1876

When the Seventh Cavalry left Fort Lincoln in May, 1876, owing to the absence of many of the Company officers who were on detached service or leave of absence, a number of changes were made temporarily. In the assignment of certain officers to companies to which they did not belong, and in the Battle of the Little Bighorn the troopers were officered as follows:

Commanding Regiment,
    Lieutenant Colonel George Armstrong Custer
Major Marcus A. Reno.
Regimental Adjutant   1st Lieutenant William Winer Cooke.
Troop A.   Captain Myles Moylan,
          1st Lieutenant Charles DeRudio,
          2nd Lieutenant Charles A. Varnum.
Troop B.   Captain Thomas M. McDougal,
          2nd Lieutenant Benjamin H. Hodgson.
Troop C.   Captain Tom W. Custer,
          2nd Lieutenant Henry M. Harrington.
Troop D.   Captain Thomas B. Weir,
          2nd Lieutenant W.S. Edgerly.

Troop E.	1st Lieutenant Algernon Smith,
	2nd Lieutenant James G. Sturgis.
Troop F.	Captain George W. Yates,
	2nd Lieutenant William Van Wyck Reily.
Troop G.	1st Lieutenant Donald McIntosh,
	2nd Lieutenant George P. Wallace.
Troop H.	Captain Frederick William Benteen,
	1st Lieutenant Frank Marion Gibson.
Troop I.	Captain Myles W. Keogh,
	2nd Lieutenant James E. Porter.
Troop K.	1st Lieutenant Edwards Godfrey,
	2nd Lieutenant Luther R. Hare.
Troop L.	1st Lieutenant James Calhoun,
	2nd Lieutenant John F. Crittenden[1].
Troop M.	Captain Thomas H. French,
	1st Lieutenant Edward C. Mathey.

Officer Biographies

Lieutenant Colonel George A. Custer born at New Rumley, Ohio, December 5, 1839. He was the eldest child of the union of Emanuel H. and Marcia [Ward] Kirkpatrick, Custer. Both of parents having been previously married and had issue therefrom. George A. Custer was appointed a cadet to the U.S. Military Academy at West Point in 1857, was graduated in 1861. He rose to the rank of Brigadier General of Volunteers and was breveted Major General in 1865. After the close of the Rebellion the regular Army was reorganized and Custer was appointed as Lieutenant Colonel in 1866, of the new regiment, Seventh Cavalry. He was killed in battle, on the Little Bighorn River, Montana—June 25th, 1876.

---

1. 20th Inf.

Major Marcus A. Reno, born in Illinois, graduated at West Point September 1, 1851. He rose to the rank of Captain in the regular Army during the Rebellion, and from January 1st to July 20th, 1865 was Colonel of the 12th Pennsylvania Volunteer Cavalry. He was appointed Major in the U.S. Seventh Cavalry December 26, 1868. For honorable service in the Rebellion he received the brevet rank of Brigadier General, of Volunteers, commanded a battalion of the Seventh Cavalry at the battle of the Little Bighorn, June 25–26, 1876. He was dismissed from the service April 1, 1880 and died at Washington, D.C. March 30, 1889.

First Lieutenant William W. Cooke, of Hamilton, Canada. served as Lieutenant in the 24th New York Cavalry during the Civil War and for gallant service received three brevet ranks, Captain, Major, and Lieutenant Colonel, mustered out June 25, 1866 and appointed 1st Lieutenant July 31, 1867. He was Regimental Adjt of the Seventh Cavalry from 1871 until his death June 25, 1876. His remains were brought back the following year, 1877, and were buried at Hamilton, Canada, where a Grand Army Post was named for him.

A TROOP

Captain Myles Moylan, Troop A. born at Amesbury, Massachusetts and enlisted in the regular Army, serving in the 2nd Dragoons until 1863. He became a Lieutenant in the 5th U.S. Cavalry from which he was dismissed October 20, 1863. He enlisted again as a private in the 4th Massachusetts Cavalry where he rose to the rank of Captain, reenlisted in the regular Army and became Sergeant Major of the Seventh Cavalry June 25, 1866, afterwards Lieutenant and, March 1, 1872 became a Captain. He retired as Major of the 10th US Cavalry April 15, 1893. He died at San Diego California Dec 11, 1909. He was married.

1st Lieutenant Camillus De Rudio, born in Italy, was a private in the New York Volunteer Infantry August 25, 1864; 2nd Lieutenant—2nd

U.S. Colored Infantry November 11, 1864. He was mustered out Jan 5, 1866; appointed 2nd Lieutenant—2nd Infantry Oct 25, 1867, assigned to 7th Cavalry July 14, 1869; 1st Lieutenant December 15, 1875; Captain, December 17, 1882, retired August 26, 1896, and was living in 1909 at Los Angeles, California.

2nd Lieutenant Charles A. Varnum, born in New York, appointed a cadet at West Point Sept 1, 1868; 2nd Lieutenant and assigned to the Seventh Cavalry June 14, 1872. He was in command of the Indian Scouts in the battle of the Little Bighorn, under Major Reno. He became 1st Lieutenant June 25, 1876; Captain, July 22, 1890; Major in 7th Cavalry February 2, 1901, and retired as Lieutenant Colonel, and was living at Orono, Maine. in 1910.

B Troop

Captain Thomas M. McDougall, born in Wisconsin; was an officer in the Civil War, was assigned to the Seventh as First Lieutenant December 31, 1870, became Captain of B Troop December 15, 1875, and with his troop acted as guard for the pack train at the battle of Little Bighorn, was retired July 22, 1890, died at Wellsville, New York July 3, 1909.

Second Lieutenant Benjamin H. Hodgson, born in Pennsylvania appointed a cadet at West Point July 1, 1865, graduated June 15, 1870 and was assigned to Seventh Cavalry as Second Lieutenant, was acting as Adjutant for Major Reno in the battle of the Little Bighorn where he was killed June 25, 1876. His remains were taken to Philadelphia for interment in July, 1877.

Captain Thomas W. Custer, born in Ohio, enlisted as private in Company Headquarters, 21st Oh. Infantry Sept 2, 1861, mustered out of the service November 24, 1865 as 2nd Lieutenant 6th Michigan Cavalry, received three brevets for gallant conduct, appointed 2nd Lieutenant 1st U.S.

Infantry February 23, 1866, 1st Lieutenant Cavalry July 28, 1866, Captain of C Troop December 2, 1875, killed at the battle of the Little Bighorn June 25, 1876. His remains were taken to the National Cemetery at Fort Leavenworth Kansas.

2nd Lieutenant Henry M. Harrington, born in New York, appointed to West Point Military Academy from Michigan, assigned as 2nd Lieutenant to the Seventh Cavalry June 14, 1872, killed at the battle of the Little Bighorn June 25, 1876. His remains were never found to be recognized. Residence Coldwater, Michigan.

D Troop

Captain Thomas B. Weir, born in Ohio, was a Second Lieutenant in the 3rd Michigan Cavalry, Oct 13, 1861, mustered out as Lieutenant Colonel February 12, 1866, appointed First Lieutenant in the Seventh Cavalry July 31, 1867 a gallant Soldier. He died in New York City December 9, 1876 while on Recruiting Service. Buried on Governors Island.

Second Lieutenant Winfield S. Edgerly, born at Farmington, New Hampshire May 29, 1846, graduated at West Point in 1870 and was assigned to the Seventh Cavalry as Second Lieutenant June 15, 1870, became First Lieutenant June 25, 1876, Major of 6th Cavalry July 9, 1898, Colonel of 2nd Cavalry February 17, 1903, retired as Brigadier General December 1909.

E Troop

First Lieutenant Algernon E. Smith, born in New York appointed 2nd Lieutenant 177th New York Infantry August 20, 1862, breveted Major for gallantry at Fort Fisher, mustered out May 15, 1865, appointed 2nd Lieutenant Seventh Cavalry August 9, 1867, 1st Lieutenant

Dec 5, 1868, was in command of E Troop when killed on the Little Bighorn June 25, 1876. Married, remains interred at Fort Leavenworth Kan. 1877.

Second Lieutenant, James Garland Sturgis, (son of Colonel S.D. Sturgis, Seventh Cavalry) born in New Mexico, graduated at West Point in 1875 and received his appointment as 2nd Lieutenant in the Seventh Cavalry June 16, 1875 and assigned to M Troop. Later on he was transferee to E Troop. He was killed in the battle on the Little Bighorn June 25, 1876. His remains were never found to be recognized, this is a fact. His brother S.D. Sturgis Jr. was in 1912 Lieutenant Colonel of the 3rd Artillery, his father died September 28, 1889.

F TROOP

Captain George W. Yates born in New York, enlisted in the 4th Michigan Infantry 1861, mustered out as First Lieutenant June 28, 1864, became a Captain in the 13th Mo—Cavalry and mustered out as such Jan 11, 1866, appointed 2nd Lieutenant in Seventh Cavalry March 26, 1866 and Captain June 12, 1867, killed in the battle at the Little Bighorn June 25, 1876, remains interred at Fort Leavenworth Kansas, married.

Second Lieutenant William Van W. Reily, born in D.C. was appointed 2nd Lieutenant in the Cavalry Oct. 15, 1875, transferee to the Seventh Cavalry January 28, 1876, killed in battle on the Little Bighorn June 25, 1876, unmarried.

G TROOP

First Lieutenant Donald McIntosh, a full blooded Indian, born in Canada, appointed from Oregon as Second Lieutenant in the Seventh Cavalry Aug. 17 1876, 1st Lieutenant March 22, 1870, was in command of G Troop at the battle of the Little Bighorn June 25, 1876 where he was killed while trying to rally his men during the retreat to the bluffs. His remains were taken to Fort Leavenworth, Kansas, but afterwards reburied at Arlington, Virginia, married.

Second Lieutenant George D. Wallace, born in South Carolina, graduated at West Point, and was assigned to the Seventh Cavalry June 14, 1872, became 1st Lieutenant June 25th, 1876, and Captain Sept 23, 1885. was killed in battle at Wounded Knee, South Dakota December 29, 1890.

H Troop

Captain, Frederick William Benteen, born in Virginia, was 1st Lieutenant of 10th Mo. Cavalry September 1, 1860, afterward Captain, Major, and Lieutenant Colonel, Colonel of 138 U.S. Colored Infantry July 15, 1865, mustered out January 6, 1866, was appointed Captain in the Seventh Cavalry July 28, 1866, Major of the 9th Cavalry December 17, 1882, retired July 7, 1888, received the brevet rank of Brigadier General for gallant service at Little Bighorn and Canyon Creek, Montana. He died June 22, 1898, married.

First Lieutenant, Francis Marion Gibson, born in Pennsylvania, appointed 2nd Lieutenant Seventh Cavalry October 5, 1867, 1st Lieutenant July 11, 1871, Captain February 5, 1880, retired December 3, 1891, was at New York City about 1908, married.

I Troop

Captain Myles W. Keogh, born at or near Carlow, Ireland, served in the Papal Zouaves, was appointed Captain of Volunteers April 9, 1862, Major and A.D.C. April 7, 1864, mustered out September 1, 1866, appointed 2nd Lieutenant 4th Cavalry May 4, 1866, Captain in Seventh Cavalry July 28, 1866, killed at the Little Bighorn, Montana June 1876. His remains were buried in Fort Hill Cemetery, Mt. Hope Lot. Auburn, New York.

First Lieutenant, James Ezekiel Porter, born in Maine, graduated at West Point, and was appointed 2nd Lieutenant in the Seventh Cavalry June 15, 1889, 1st Lieutenant March 1st, 1872, killed in battle at the Little Bighorn, June 25, 1876, body not recognized.

K Troop

First Lieutenant, Edward Settle Godfrey, born in Ohio, Private in Co. D 21st Ohio Infantry April 26, to August 12, 1861, Cadet at West Point July 1, 1863, 2nd Lieutenant Seventh Cavalry June 17, 1867, 1st Lieutenant February 1, 1868, Captain December 9, 1876, Major 1st Cavalry December 8, 1896, transferee to Seventh Cavalry January 7, 1897, Lieutenant Colonel 12th Cavalry February 2, 1901, Colonel 9th Cavalry June 26, 1901, was breveted Major February 27, 1890 for gallant service at Bear Paw Mountain, retired as Brigadier General, was living at Cookstown, New Jersey in 1914.

Second Lieutenant Luther Rector Hare, born in Indiana, graduated at West Point, was appointed 2nd Lieutenant in the Seventh Cavalry June 17, 1874, 1st Lieutenant June 25, 1876, Captain December 29, 1890, Major of 12th Cavalry February 2, 1901, retired, and resided at Austin, Texas 1913.

L Troop

First Lieutenant James Calhoun, born in Ohio, Private and Sergeant in Company D 22nd New York Infantry February 22, 1865, 2nd Lieutenant in the 32nd Infantry 1867, transferee to 21st Infantry. April 19, 1869, assigned to Seventh Cavalry January 1, 1871, 1st Lieutenant January 9, 1871, married Margaret Custer. He was killed at the Little Bighorn June 25, 1876, no issue, remains buried at Fort Leavenworth Kansas.

Second Lieutenant John F. Crittenden, born in Kentucky a son of General T.L. Crittenden, (CO—17th Infantry). He was appointed as 2nd Lieutenant in the 20th Infantry October 15, 1875, was at his own request, assigned to the Seventh Cavalry for the Campaign of 1876. He was killed at the Little Bighorn June 25, 1876, and at his father's request his remains were left where he fell.

M TROOP

Captain Thomas Henry French, born in Maryland, Private in the 10th U.S. Infantry January 13 to June 9, 1864, 2nd Lieutenant 10th Infantry, 1st Lieutenant June 23, 1864, Captain March 28, 1868, assigned to Seventh Cavalry January 1, 1871, retired February 5, 1880. He died at Fort Leavenworth, Kansas March 27, 1882, remains were afterwards taken to Baltimore, Maryland by a Sister, was unmarried.

First Lieutenant Edward Gustave Mathey, born in France. 1st Sergeant Company C 17th Ind Volunteer Infantry May 31, 1861, 2nd Lieutenant 1862, rose to the rank of Major in the Civil War and was mustered out June 13, 1865, appointed 2nd Lieutenant Seventh Cavalry September 24, 1867, 1st Lieutenant May 10, 1870, Captain September 30, 1877, retired with the rank of Lieutenant Colonel December 11, 1896, resided at Denver Colorado 1912.

SURGEONS

Dr. J.M. DeWolf, killed on Reno's Hill, June 25th, 1876.

Dr. G.E. Lord, killed with Custer's command, June 25th, 1876.

Dr. H.R. Porter, died.

General Gibbon's Expedition of 1876
THE MONTANA COLUMN

consisted of:

General John Gibbon,[1] Colonel of the Seventh Infantry, and Staff.

First Lieutenant J.W. Jacobs, Regt-Quartermaster.

Lieutenant L.F. Barnett, Regt Adjutant. 3 Officers.

Surgeon, Dr. Paulding

Major James S. Brisbin,[2] commanding Battalion of the Second Cavalry.

Four Troops, 10 Officers, 186 men.

Captain Henry B. Freeman, commanding Battalion of the Seventh Infantry

Six Companies.   13 Officers, 220 men.

Non Combatants, 1 Officer, 20 men

Crow Indian Scouts, two Interpreters and one guide, 26 men.

Total—27 Officers, 432 men.

*   *   *

Lieutenant C.A. Woodruff of the Seventh Infantry, was in command of a Battery of Two Gatling Guns, and one 12 Pound Napoleon manned by a detachment of the Seventh Infantry.

*   *   *

Lieutenant J.H. Bradley, Seventh Infantry was chief of Scouts, his command consisting of a detail of mounted Infantry and the Crow Indians.

Officers of the Second Cavalry

With General Gibbon, 1876

James S. Brisbin, Major commanding Battalion.

[Major Brisbin had been a Brigadier General of Volunteers,] he died January 14, 1892

Troop F.	Captain.	[absent]
" "	1st Lieutenant.	[absent]
" "	2nd Lieutenant.	Charles F. Roe commanding the Troop resigned in 1889. Major General New York National Guard in 1912.

---

1. Died February 6, 1896, at sixty-nine.
2. Died January 14, 1892.

Troop G.   Captain James N. Wheelan. Lieutenant Colonel 7th Cav-
                alry 1899. retired.

"   "   1st Lieutenant Gustave C Doane. died on May 5, 1892.

"   "   2nd Lieutenant Edward McClernand. Engineer Officer
                for Gibbon command. Retired as Brigadier General, was
                living in Pennsylvania in 1912. [Easton]

"   H.   Captain Edward Ball. Retired as Major of 7th Cavalry, he
                died October 22, 1884.

"   "   1st Lieutenant, James G. MacAdams. died June 1890.

"   "   2nd Lieutenant [absent, Lovell H. Jerome]

"   L.   Captain. Lewis Thompson. committed suicide on the Yel-
                lowstone, July 19, 1876.

"   "   1st Lieutenant Samuel T. Hamilton retired as Captain.
                Died.

"   "   2nd Lieutenant. Charles B. Scofield. died in Cuba Feb. 2,
                1901

                        *   *   *

Officers of the Seventh Infantry with General Gibbon's command:

Co. A. Captain Wm. A. Logan, killed in battle August 9, 1877.

                1st Lieutenant Charles A. Coolidge, retired as Brigadier
                General resided at Detroit Michigan 1912.

                2nd Lieutenant Francis Woodbridge, retired in 1891, died
                April 22, 1891.

Co. B. Captain, Thaddeus S. Kirtland, retired 1906 July 1891 as Major, died
                at Chicago November 30, 1906.

                1st Lieutenant. James H. Bradley, killed in battle Aug. 9,
                1877.

                2nd Lieutenant Charles A. Booth, retired Colonel, resided
                at 1856 Ontario Place, Washington DC. 1913.

Co. E. Captain Walter Clifford, died February 23, 1883.

                1st Lieutenant, absent 1876.

2nd Lieutenant George S. Young, Colonel. 21st Infantry 1913. Vancouver Barracks, Washington

Co. K. Captain James M.J. Sanno. Colonel. 18th Infantry, 1899.
1st Lieutenant, 2nd Lieutenant

Co. H. Captain Henry B Freeman, retired, Brigadier General. 1916 La Bonte, Wyoming
1st Lieutenant. Charles A. Woodruff. retired. Brigadier General. 1913 Veterans Home, California
2nd Lieutenant. Frederick M.H. Kendrick, retired in 1900. Major. —

Co. I. Captain [Charles C. Rawn, absent sick] died October 6, 1887.
1st Lieutenant Wm. L. English, died from wounds August 20, 1877. 2nd Lieutenant.

Suggested Reading

Bourke, John G. *On the Border with Crook*. New York: C. Scribner's Sons, 1891. Reprinted. Columbus, Ohio: Long's College Book Co., 1950.

Bradley, Lieutenant James H. "Journal of the Sioux Campaign of 1876." *Montana Historical Society Contributions*, vol. 2, 1896. Reprinted with additional materials: *The March of the Montana Column: A Prelude to the Custer Disaster*. Norman: University of Oklahoma Press, 1961.

Brady, Cyrus Townsend. *Indian Fights and Fighters*. New York: Doubleday, Page and Co., 1904.

Brininstool, E. A. *Troopers with Custer*. Mechanicsburg, Pa.: Stackpole Books, 1952.

Carroll, John. *Custer in Texas: An Interrupted Narrative*. New York: Sol Lewis and Liveright, 1975.

Connell, Evan S. *Son of the Morning Star*. San Francisco: North Point Press, 1984.

Custer, Elizabeth B. *Boots and Saddles: or Life in Dakota with General Custer*. Norman and London: University of Oklahoma Press, 1987.

Custer, George Armstrong. *My Life on the Plains; or Personal Experiences with Indians*, ed. Edgar I. Stewart. Norman: University of Oklahoma Press, 1962.

DuMont, John S. *The Custer Battle Guns*. Fort Collins, Colo.: Old Army Press, 1974.

Finerty, John F. *War-Path and Bivouac or The Conquest of the Sioux*. Norman: University of Oklahoma Press, 1977. [Originally published in 1890.]

Frost, Lawrence A. *The Custer Album: A Pictorial History of General George A. Custer*. Norman and London: University of Oklahoma Press, 1990.

Graham, W. A. *The Custer Myth: A Source Book of Custeriana*. Harrisburg, Pa.: Stackpole Co., 1953.

Gray, John S. *Centennial Campaign: The Sioux War of 1876*. Fort Collins, Colo.: Old Army Press, 1976.

———. *Custer's Last Campaign*. Lincoln and London: University of Nebraska Press, 1991.

Grinnell, George B. *The Cheyenne Indians*. New Haven, Conn., 1923.

———. *The Fighting Cheyennes*. New York: Charles Scribner's Sons, 1915.

Hammer, Kenneth, ed. *Custer in '76: Walter Camp's Notes on the Custer Fight*. Provo, Utah: Brigham Young University Press, 1976.

Hanson, J. M. *The Conquest of the Missouri: Being the Story and the Life and Exploits of Grant Marsh*. New York: Murray Hill Books, Inc., 1946.

Hardorff, Richard. *Custer Battle Casualties*. El Segundo, Calif.: Upton & Sons, Publishers, 1991.

Hubbard, E. *The Custer Battle. The Teepee Book*. In two volumes, compiled and edited by J. M. Carroll. New York: Sol Lewis. (Reprinted from the original June 1915 *Teepee Book* 1 [6], Herbert Coffeen, ed.)

Hughes, Col. Robert P. "The Campaign Against the Sioux." *Journal of the Military Service Institution of the United States* vol. 18 (January 1896).

Katz, Mark. *Custer in Photographs*. Gettysburg, Pa.: Yo-Mark Production Co., 1985.

King, W. Kent. *Massacre: The Custer Cover-up*. El Segundo, Calif.: Upton & Sons, 1989.

Libby, Orin Grant, ed. *The Arikara Narrative of the Campaign Against the Hostile Dakotas, 1876*. North Dakota Historical Collections, VI. Bismarck, 1920.

Luther, Tal. *Custer High Spots*. Fort Collins, Colo.: Old Army Press, 1972.

McLaughlin, James. *My Friend the Indian*. Lincoln: Bison Books, University of Nebraska Press, 1989.

Marquis, Thomas B. *Keep the Last Bullet for Yourself*. New York: Two Continents Publishing Group, 1976.

Merington, Marguerite. *The Custer Story: The Life and Intimate Letters of General George A. Custer and His Wife Elizabeth*. Lincoln and London: University of Nebraska Press, 1987.

Miller, David Humphries. *Custer's Fall: The Indian Side of the Story*. Lincoln and London: University of Nebraska Press, 1957.

Monaghan, Jay. *The Life of George Armstrong Custer*. Boston: Little, Brown and Company, 1959.

Reedstrom, Ernest L. *Bugles, Banners & War Bonnets: From Fort Riley to the Little Big Horn: A Study of Lt. Col. George Armstrong Custer's 7th Cavalry, the Soldiers, Their Weapons and Equipment*. Caldwell, Idaho: Caxton Printers, 1977.

Roe, C. F. General Roe's Narrative. In *Custer's Last Battle*, ed. Robert Bruce, 8–18. New York: National Highway Association, 1927.

Roosevelt, Theodore. *Ranch Life and the Hunting Trail*. New York: Century, 1888.

Sarf, Wayne Michael. *The Little Bighorn Campaign*. Conshohocken, Pa.: Combined Books, 1993.

Stewart, Edgar I. *Custer's Luck*. Norman: University of Oklahoma Press, 1955.

Terrell, John Upton, and Col. George Walton. *Faint the Trumpet Sounds*. New York: David McKay Company, 1966.

Urwin, Gregory J. W. *Custer Victorious: The Civil War Battles of George Armstrong Custer*. Lincoln and London: University of Nebraska Press, 1990.

Utley, Robert M. *Cavalier in Buckskin: George Armstrong Custer and the Western Frontier*. Norman: University of Oklahoma Press, 1988.

————. *Frontier Regulars: The United States Army and the Indian, 1866–1890.* New York: Macmillan Publishing Co., 1973.

————, ed. *The Reno Court of Inquiry: The Chicago Times Account.* Fort Collins, Colo.: Old Army Press, 1972.

Whittaker, Frederick A. *A Complete Life of Major General George A. Custer.* New York: Sheldon & Co., 1876.

The hills that have watched afar
The valleys ablaze with war
        Shall look on the tasselled corn;
And the dust of the grinded grain,
Instead of the blood of the slain,
        Shall sprinkle thy banks, Big Horn!

The Ute and the wandering Crow
Shall know as the white men know,
        And fare as the white men fare;
The pale and the red shall be brothers,
One's rights shall be as another's,
        Home, School, and House of Prayer!

O mountains that climb to snow,
O river winding below,
        Through meadows by war once trod,
O wild waste lands that await
The harvest exceeding great,
        Break forth into praise of God!

"Ha-nul-la".
(It is finished)

FOR THE BEST IN PAPERBACKS, LOOK FOR THE

In every corner of the world, on every subject under the sun, Penguin represents quality and variety—the very best in publishing today.

For complete information about books available from Penguin—including Puffins, Penguin Classics, and Arkana—and how to order them, write to us at the appropriate address below. Please note that for copyright reasons the selection of books varies from country to country.

In the United Kingdom: Please write to *Dept. JC, Penguin Books Ltd, FREEPOST, West Drayton, Middlesex UB7 0BR.*

If you have any difficulty in obtaining a title,.please send your order with the correct money, plus ten percent for postage and packaging, to *P.O. Box No. 11, West Drayton, Middlesex UB7 0BR*

In the United States: Please write to *Consumer Sales, Penguin USA, P.O. Box 999, Dept. 17109, Bergenfield, New Jersey 07621-0120.* VISA and MasterCard holders call 1-800-253-6476 to order all Penguin titles

In Canada: Please write to *Penguin Books Canada Ltd, 10 Alcorn Avenue, Suite 300, Toronto, Ontario M4V 3B2*

In Australia: Please write to *Penguin Books Australia Ltd, P.O. Box 257, Ringwood, Victoria 3134*

In New Zealand: Please write to *Penguin Books (NZ) Ltd, Private Bag 102902, North Shore Mail Centre, Auckland 10*

In India: Please write to *Penguin Books India Pvt Ltd, 706 Eros Apartments, 56 Nehru Place, New Delhi 110 019*

In the Netherlands: Please write to *Penguin Books Netherlands bv, Postbus 3507, NL-1001 AH Amsterdam*

In Germany: Please write to *Penguin Books Deutschland GmbH, Metzlerstrasse 26, 60594 Frankfurt am Main*

In Spain: Please write to *Penguin Books S. A., Bravo Murillo 19, 1° B, 28015 Madrid*

In Italy: Please write to *Penguin Italia s.r.l., Via Felice Casati 20, I-20124 Milano*

In France: Please write to *Penguin France S. A., 17 rue Lejeune, F−31000 Toulouse*

In Japan: Please write to *Penguin Books Japan, Ishikiribashi Building, 2−5−4, Suido, Bunkyo-ku, Tokyo 112*

In Greece: Please write to *Penguin Hellas Ltd, Dimocritou 3, GR−106 71 Athens*

In South Africa: Please write to *Longman Penguin Southern Africa (Pty) Ltd, Private Bag X08, Bertsham 2013*